The First Karmapa

The First Karmapa

The Life and Teachings of Dusum Khyenpa

Foreword by His Holiness the 17th Karmapa, Ogyen Trinley Dorje

Translated by David Karma Choephel and Michele Martin

KTD Publications
Woodstock, New York
A Karmapa 900 Publication

Homage to the One who Embodies the Activity of all the Buddhas

KTD Publications
335 Meads Mountain Road
Woodstock, NY 12498, USA
www.KTDPublications.org

A Karmapa 900 Publication

Cover drawing by Amji Dawa, drawn according to instructions given by His Holiness the 17th Karmapa

Cover design by Louise Light (www.louiselight.net)

Printed in the U.S.A.

ISBN 978-1-934608-32-6
LCCN 2012932385

CONTENTS

Foreword

by His Holiness the Seventeenth Karmapa
Ogyen Trinley Dorje

The First Karmapa, Dusum Khyenpa, was famous as the first person in history to reincarnate in a recognizable way so that he could continue caring for his disciples. This collection of teachings and biographies allows us to see what is less well known: how someone could develop a skillful compassion so intense it crossed even the normal boundaries of death and rebirth.

This book was originally compiled to commemorate the 900th birth anniversary of Dusum Khyenpa, the First Karmapa. The main aim of this book, as well as of the Karmapa 900 commemorations, is to allow us all to come closer to Dusum Khyenpa and to feel his kindness to us. Among the teachings included in this book are records of oral discourses that Dusum Khyenpa gave to large gatherings. As we read them, we can overcome the separation of time and take a seat alongside his direct disciples, tasting with them the flavor of the exquisite nectar of Dusum Khyenpa's Dharma. In this way, we can deepen our connection to the First Karmapa as a masterful teacher of Dharma, and to the lineage that he founded as he taught.

By receiving his teachings and reflecting on his deeds, we

can experience his boundless compassion and loving-kindness for all sentient beings, and marvel at the magnificent path he followed as a bodhisattva. As we do so, we naturally feel a sense of wonder and gratitude. The way for us to enact this gratitude is to contemplate his virtuous qualities and seek to develop them within ourselves. This is the best step we can take towards repaying the First Karmapa's tremendous kindness to us.

The kindness of Dusum Khyenpa was the kindness of a perfectly wise and compassionate guru. For Buddhism in general and the tantric path in particular, spiritual teachers are of tremendous importance. We cannot find Buddha Shakyamuni living amongst us today and so cannot receive teachings from him directly. But we do have spiritual friends and gurus who perform the functions of a buddha in our lives. They give us teachings and indicate the proper way to practice, and thus are like second buddhas for us. Gurus are incalculably kind to us.

When we speak of gurus, we generally distinguish between lineage and root gurus. The First Karmapa, Dusum Khyenpa, is the lineage guru who established the Karma Kagyu lineage. He is a lineage guru also in the sense that he is the wellspring of the long and unbroken series of masters and disciples who passed this Karma Kagyu lineage from one to the other in what we call the Golden Rosary. All the goodness that these masters created in the world over the past 900 years can be traced to the original kindness of Dusum Khyenpa.

At the same time, the First Karmapa is also the root guru of all who practice in the Karma Kagyu tradition. Since he has been returning in an uninterrupted line of incarnations for 900 years, his bodhisattva activities have been revealed to us unceasingly. In this way, the First Karmapa, Dusum Khyenpa, is the embodiment of all the root and lineage gurus of the Karma Kagyu.

Starting with Dusum Khyenpa, all the reincarnations of the Karmapa have vowed to come back continually to sustain their enlightened activity for the benefit of all sentient beings. The force that motivates that vow is nothing other than the boundless compassion and wisdom that Dusum Khyenpa first generated nearly 900 years ago.

Through his infinite compassion, he nurtures a constant wish to help all sentient beings free themselves of suffering and attain happiness, and along with this is a willingness to sacrifice himself under any circumstance. Through his immeasurable wisdom, he points out the right path so that all beings may eliminate the darkness of their ignorance, and he helps them attain the utmost joy. These two qualities of compassion and wisdom represent the very nature of the Karmapa and, indeed, the spirit of Buddhism.

Yet it is crucial to recognize that compassion and wisdom are not something that only the Karmapas have, for within every ordinary person, the seed of such qualities is present. If you are diligent and persevere, as Dusum Khyenpa did, you are equally capable of accomplishing the enormous task of benefiting all beings, and at the same time, you yourself will also experience limitless, supreme joy.

I sincerely aspire that this book may awaken readers all around the world to the presence of the seeds of perfect goodness that lie within everyone. The aim of all the deeds and teachings of the First Karmapa was to nurture and bring to fruition these seeds within us. Therefore, as a means of supporting the fulfillment of Dusum Khyenpa's aspirations for sentient beings, I am pleased that this book is now available in English translation.

This book contains both Dusum Khyenpa's spiritual biography and his Dharma teachings. Nevertheless, I feel that the biography of Dusum Khyenpa is itself also a teaching. In fact, I believe the life a lama lives is the greatest instruction to the students who follow him or her. It is an instruction we can actually see. The lama's deeds display the Dharma in action for us. They can instruct our hearts with the fullness of lived experience. In the lama's actions, we can observe how the Dharma becomes Dharma and how that Dharma becomes a path. We can watch how the path eliminates confusion, and how confusion arises as wisdom.

Reading the life story of Dusum Khyenpa can inspire us to emulate his character and the qualities of his body, speech, and mind. Reading his teachings, we gain practical guidance in how to do so. In a sense, his or her life is the most direct and effective teaching that a guru can give a disciple. The more attention we pay to our gurus' actions and outlook, the more we can fulfill their aspirations, and the more our minds can merge with theirs. In this way, when we remember Dusum Khyenpa's deeds and kindness, we are not commemorating an ordinary being. Rather, we are regarding his acts and teachings as a transmission from the buddhas and bodhisattvas.

I aspire that you receive fully the transmission that is offered to you by this book. As you read Dusum Khyenpa's teachings and his spiritual biographies, I hope that you will deepen your resolve and courage to transform yourself into a great being like him, who can bring perfect benefit to yourself and countless others.

Translators' Introduction

Dusum Khyenpa (1110–1193) was widely recognized in his own time as a realized master of the Kagyu lineage. From an early age, he spent several decades devoting himself to study and meditation under the guidance of spiritual friends in the Kadampa tradition and then under Kagyu masters, especially the peerless Gampopa. A child of the mountains, Dusum Khyenpa spent many years meditating in isolated retreats. He developed meditative experience, refined his realization, asked questions of his lama, and then went back into retreat to meditate further. Reading the stories of his life in the spiritual biographies as well as in the songs and dialogues, one can see the diligence, devotion, and single-minded dedication that led to Dusum Khyenpa being recognized as one of the greatest masters of his time and for all the generations since.

Most of the stories are found in the five spiritual biographies that make up more than half of this volume. They have been interleaved with his teachings, songs, and dialogues to give a fuller sense of who he was. Each biography brings its own special flavor and accent, and though they may repeat a story, tell it differently, or even contradict each other, they all contribute to presenting a fuller portrait of Dusum Khyenpa.

The authors of the biographies were mostly close disciples of Dusum Khyenpa and often quote him directly. *The Golden Isle* and *the Spiritual Biography in Verse* were written by Galo, who was both a student and a teacher of Dusum Khyenpa. *The Golden Isle* is the most literary and elegant of the five texts. *The Spiritual Biography in Verse* is for devoted students to memorize so they can recall the main events of his life. *A String of Jewels* was written by Dechungwa, who interviewed two of Dusum Khyenpa's main monks and selected mostly the visionary or miraculous stories for his account. *Dusum Khyenpa's Life Story in One Hundred and Eight Vignettes*—the longest version and based on the images in a painting—was composed by Bhikshu Kumara Bodhi, known in the texts as Shönnu. He was asked by Dusum Khyenpa to stay on and look after the representations of the master's body, speech, and mind after he passed away. In the text itself, Shönnu relates that he worked extensively on the glorious Drepung Stupa built to enshrine the body of Dusum Khyenpa. Many of the accounts in *The Final Words* are exactly the same as those in the *Vignettes*, and we can assume that Kumara Bodhi (or someone using his text) contributed here as well. These records of Dusum Khyenpa's life thus come from those who knew him very well based on their own direct experience of his life and teachings. We are fortunate that they have survived for these nine hundred years.

To a Western reader, these spiritual biographies may seem a bit unusual, for they do not relate the normal events we would expect; rather, they tell of how a master studied, practiced, and attained realization. Events and their details are selected based on what contributed to a lama's spiritual path. Indeed the Tibetan word for this genre is *nam thar* (*rnam thar*), "liberation." These accounts take for granted the existence of past and future lives, the master's knowledge of them, and many other extraordinary powers. There are also many lists of disciples' and teachers' names, the practices they did, and the empowerments they received, revealing the shape of the lama's life and how the teachings were passed down in an unbroken lineage. They show the relationship between masters and disciples over lifetimes and create a connection to the future and the past, all the way back to the Indian masters, such as Saraha, Maitripa, and Telopa, the sources of the Kagyu Dharma. Reading about how these relationships developed can also inspire us to undertake our own path to full awakening.

Interwoven with the spiritual lives are the words of Dusum Khyenpa himself. Two of the texts, *A Strand of Pearls* and the *Dharma Talks*, are transcriptions of teachings that Dusum Khyenpa gave orally. In the first of these, Dusum Khyenpa explains how to take refuge, make dedications, and practice the discipline of the daylong fasting vows—three practices that provide an essential support for meditation training. They are given in the form of instructions to a master about how to perform these rituals, but they also provide essential advice for anyone doing these practices.

The *Dharma Talks* speak more directly about meditation practice. These are part of a genre called *tsok chö* (*tshogs chos*), which literally means "Dharma for the gathering"—oral teachings given by a great master to a group. They tell aspiring meditators what is needed for practice, what kind of an attitude to take, and what problems or mistakes to avoid. Above all they stress the importance of practicing now while we have the opportunity in the midst of this transient and uncertain human life.

Also included in this book are the spiritual songs of Dusum Khyenpa and his *Dialogues with Gampopa*. The *Collection of Songs* gathers supplications to great masters of the past, expressions of devotion to his lama, songs of joy and wonder at finding realization, and even some verses of bemused disgust at his own weaknesses. The *Dialogues with Gampopa* are Dusum Khyenpa's own record of the conversations he had with Gampopa as the latter guided him through his practice. Ranging from discussions of *chandali* (*tummo*) and others of the six yogas to questions about meditative experiences and his realization of the nature of mind, the *Dialogues* are like a window onto the increasingly subtle insights that come through advanced meditation.

Although the original Tibetan book presented all the spiritual biographies in the first half and the teachings in the second half, here the life stories and songs are alternated in hopes that this will give the reader a better appreciation not just of the teachings that Dusum Khyenpa gave but of the example he provided with his life.[1] The two go hand in hand. In the Dharma talks, he tells us that it is important to follow a genuine teacher, and in the spiritual biographies he shows us how to do it. He tells us to put aside worldly affairs and meditate, and he demonstrates how he himself disregarded hardship and difficulty for the sake of practice.

In these texts, Dusum Khyenpa is referred to as Rinpoche, master, and Khampa Gray Hair or Lama Gray Hair, but not once is he called the Karmapa. Only when he came back, identified himself to his students, and resumed his activity did he become known in retrospect as the First Karmapa. By returning, he established the tradition of *tulkus*, or reincarnate lamas, coming back lifetime after lifetime—a practice he has continued now for seventeen lives, manifesting all kinds of activity to meet the varying needs and situations of sentient beings in different eras.

We hope that all those who encounter this book will be able to follow Dusum Khyenpa's example to whatever extent they are able so that they too may go, in his words, "from light to light and happiness to happiness with the yidams and dakinis coming to welcome them."

1. Dus gsum mkhyen pa, *dPal ldan dus gsum mkhyen pa'i zhal gdams bces btus* (Kalimpong, West Bengal, India: Rigpe Dorje Institute), 2010.

Acknowledgments

We would like to thank the people who have helped us prepare this translation. First and foremost we are grateful to Khenchen Thrangu Rinpoche, who, with his vast knowledge, answered our most difficult questions. We would also like to thank Khenpo Losal, Khenpo Sherap Phuntsok, and the other khenpos of the Vajra Vidya Institute for carefully going over many difficult or unclear passages in the text. Special thanks are due to Gen Nyima Tsering, who gave freely of his time and expertise to clarify many details, particularly in the spiritual lives. Thanks also go to Tracy Davis for her excellent copyediting. All of their kind support made possible a translation that we hope is accurate, understandable, and inspiring. For anything mistaken or unclear that may remain, we request the reader's forbearance.

Supplication

NAMO GURU

We supplicate Lord Vajradhara
In the supreme realm of Akanishta,
Where the dharma expanse and wisdom have
  the same taste:
Bless us children who supplicate you.

We supplicate Lord Telopa
In the retreat of Shri Nagaracha.
You mastered the Dharma of the four oral lineages:
Bless us children who supplicate you.

We supplicate Lord Naropa
In the retreat of Pullahari in the north.
You mastered the Dharma of texts and letters:
Bless us children who supplicate you.

We supplicate Lord Marpa the Translator
In the retreat of Shinglo Grove in the south.
You mastered all of the Dharma of the tantras:
Bless us children who supplicate you

We supplicate Lord Milarepa
In a retreat of snow and ice.

You mastered the Dharma of mixing and transference:
Bless us children who supplicate you.

We supplicate the Lord Physician of Dakpo
In the monastery of glorious Daklha in the east.
You mastered the Dharma of mahamudra:
Bless us children who supplicate you.

We supplicate the body of Lord Gomtsul
In the monastery of Lhalung Pal.
You have the experience of seeing the Dharma nakedly:
Bless us children who supplicate you.

We supplicate the lamas
On lotus and moon seats above our crowns.
You point out our minds as the dharmakaya:
Bless us children who supplicate you.

We supplicate the mother Vajra Varahi
In the palace of Uddiyana in the west.
You have mastery of the supreme and ordinary:
Bless us children who supplicate you.

We supplicate the glorious guardian pair
In the place of the great charnel ground.
You have mastery over the four activities:
Bless us children who supplicate you.

May our supplication to you
Remove completely every obscuration
For us and all beings in the six realms:
May we become your equals in glorious qualities.

Spoken by Dusum Khyenpa.

The Golden Isle

The Precious Lives of the Lord of Dharma
in Eighteen Chapters

I pay homage to the Omniscient One.

The nature of your great knowing blazes like the sun;
Your love shines like the light of the moon.
I bow to you with the crowns
Of bodies as numerous as all atoms.
I gather the words of the great one about ten emanations in the past,
Five in the present, and three in the future.

In the beginning, glorious Dusum Khyenpa gave rise to bodhichitta. In the middle, he traveled the five paths and gathered the two accumulations. In the end, he discovered unsurpassed full awakening, through which he will continually engage in enlightened activity until all the karma of living beings is exhausted.

Chapter One: The Former Life in the Pure Land of Beryl Blue

He remembered, "In a previous time I took birth in a world realm known as Beryl Blue. There are many stories about this."

Chapter Two: The Former Life on an Island

"Once I was born on the island of Dharitha, located between the southern continent of the Rose Apple and the western continent of the Bountiful Cow. Gampopa lived there as the yogi Surapa. I received from him both aspirational and engaged bodhichitta."

Chapter Three: The Former Life at the Edge of the Rose Apple Continent

"Once, in a place called Tartita to the west of the southern continent of the Rose Apple, I was a natural yogi without a master. Belonging to the caste of smiths and named Antita, I practiced with great diligence in mountain retreats and solitary places."

Chapter Four: The Former Life on the Continent of the Bountiful Cow

"I took another birth on the western continent of the Bountiful Cow as a Brahmin named Dharma Atita. My secret name was Dharmashri. I received key instructions from Lama Telopa and benefited a number of living beings."

Chapter Five: The Former Life as an Elephant

About a later birth, he said, "Our present-day patron, Kya Gönpawa, had taken birth again in the west of the western continent of the Bountiful Cow as the king Dharmashri, a non-Buddhist tyrant who was harming his kingdom. In order to tame him, I took birth among his animals and lived as a very powerful elephant in a herd of seven hundred. Once, with a large troop of soldiers, the king went out on the road riding that great elephant, and it trampled him to death. For several lifetimes, I have led this king into the practice of virtue."

Chapter Six: The Former Life at the Far Edge of the Rose Apple Continent

"I took birth in the far northeastern corner of the Rose Apple Continent by a river known as Adorned with Lotus Flowers. I was known as Bhikshu Dharmakirti and my abbot was the Brahmin Sajjana. I supplicated the master Dombipa, who lived under a rock overhang in the mountains. I was also the abbot for four students: Geshe Tsöndru Sherap, Rinchen Gyaltsen, Dok Khepa, and Menge Josey. Geshe Chapa was born as a minor pandita and acted as my master. Geshe Dorje Senge was a student of Chapa and has taken another birth near him."

Chapter Seven: The Former Life in the Country of Kalingka

"Then, I took birth as King Dawa Nampar Nönpa in the land of Kalingka. My teacher was a previous incarnation of Gampopa, Master Sangye Yeshe Shap. And his master was Jampal Shenyen Avadhuti, an incarnation of Milarepa." In contrast to the account in the Guhyasamaja, here, the king was on his way to circumambulate the glorious Drepung Stupa in the south of India when he heard a voice from the sky say, "You have not yet attained siddhis. Go back and gather the conditioned roots of goodness." So he established a monastery there for many monks and amassed a great amount of conditioned virtue. He circumambulated the stupa numerous times and attained all the ordinary siddhis.

When he left, two dogs who followed him also attained ordinary siddhis. He commented, "Now they have been reborn in Uddiyana as two worldly dakinis who are rougher than the others."

Dusum Khyenpa continued, "There are many people here from the retinue of this king and also from Kartika and Samey. Although they no longer have them, at that time both Tönpa Sangye and Geshe Rinchen Gyaltsen had numerous ordinary siddhis."

Then he was asked, "Why don't they have them now?"

"The siddhis came from the practice they did during that period.

"At this time, the supplications of thirteen of you—some of whom supplicated earlier and some later—were fulfilled. From among Tönpa Sangye, Rinchen Gyaltsen, Yönten Ö,

Yönten Lama, Gendun Drak, and Mönlam Lama, one is in Ü and one is in Tre."

Chapter Eight: The Former Life in Uddiyana

"Afterward, I took birth in Uddiyana in the west central area of the Rose Apple Continent. Known as Shiladanti, I was a disciple of Telopa and a yogi of supreme ability who stayed in groves and forests. From that time, there are four students here to whom I gave empowerments: Dorje Bum, Gomngön, Shakya Sherap, and Gompa Chöpal."

Chapter Nine: The Former Life on the Eastern Continent of Supreme Body

"After that, I was born on the eastern continent of Supreme Body as Sherap Sangmo, the daughter of King Gewa Sangpo and of her mother, Sherap Chenma. (I was worried that I would have had to rule the kingdom if I had been born a son.) My secret name was Tsokye Jangchup and my parents died when I was young. Later I met Gampopa, who had then incarnated as Bhikshu Dharmasiddhi, and offered him a large portion of my possessions. I received from him a lay woman's vows, for which I followed the precepts correctly. At that time, many of you along with numerous friends were present. When we were gathering merit, you were seven brothers, whose father was Kusala Kirti and mother, Kusala Bhadri. You are now Gendun Ö, Sherap Lama, Mönlam Lama, Yönten Ö, Yeshe Ö, Yeshe Öser, and one other. The first three also helped to protect my life."

Chapter Ten: The Former Life on an Island, Concluding the Account of Past Lives

"In the life previous to this one, between the eastern continent of Supreme Body and the southern continent of the Rose Apple, I was born on a nameless island in a city called Ratapa or Rajaphala, also known as the City of the Excellent King. My father was Dharmagupta, who belonged to the merchant caste, and my mother was Sumati. I was called Pratikirti and lived to the age of one hundred sixty-four.

"At that time, Gampopa was Palgyi Bepa, and I received from him three sadhanas: Mahamaya, Tara the Wish-Fulfilling Wheel, and Vajrasattva. I explained this Tara practice to ten people who are now Yönten Ö, Gendun Ö, Yeshe Lama, Mönlam Lama, Jungne Lama, Gyaltsen Lama, Tsangtön Tsulseng, Tre Geshe Könchok Pal, Dorje Sherap, and a Kadampa as well. When I was attending a feast offering with Gampopa, about twenty of you were present, including Geshe Kadampa, Master Rinchen Gyaltsen, Tönpa Sangye, two attendants, Gendun Drak, Mönlam Lama, Dorje Sherap, Geshe Könchok Pal, and Tönpa Tsulseng. Two nuns were also there; one is here in this place and the other has taken birth in Ü. Since the patron Gönpawa was the son of a wealthy householder, he served as a sponsor. Having made a connection then and taken this rebirth, he is a sponsor here and will also be one later.

"Abbot Kadrakpa twice served as my abbot. In that life, I was Bhikshu Ratnashila. As a yogi endowed with the ability to practice yogic discipline, I benefited disciples, Kadampas and others, again and again through the various categories of explanations and empowerments. To Geshe Sanak, Geshe Yulbarwa, and another person, I gave refuge and the vows of engaged bodhichitta. One of them, who did not keep the precepts, has now taken birth right here. The great abbot was a pandita to whom I explained the bodhisattva levels and *The Twenty Stanzas on the Vows*.

"Geshe Lama Ö took an excellent rebirth in Domey Setsang near India where a master from his previous life is staying. He could be called a siddha."

Chapter Eleven: The Years of Undergoing Hardship and Benefiting Others

In this present life, Dusum Khyenpa was born in the region of Treshö known as Pochu Lhadong Karpo on the north side of the Rose Apple Continent, which is to the south of the center of this World of Enduring Suffering. His father was Gompa Pal, his mother was the daughter of Mingdren, and he was named Gepel. At the age of eleven, he practiced Palden Lhamo and saw her clearly. Then he subdued his enemy.

He wanted to benefit others during this time when the reflection of the Buddha's teachings was still present here, during the ten periods of five hundred years.[1] So at the age of sixteen he took novice vows in Kadrak with Geshe Chokgi Lama, whom he served for two years. From Geshe Trarawa he received the empowerment of Chakrasamvara and then heard teachings on Achala and also on the Kadampa tradition. At the age of nineteen, he traveled to the region of Central Tibet, and at twenty, he arrived at Yulthang in

Tölung. With Geshe Gyamar and Chapa he studied the main texts of the three Madhyamikas from the east[2] as well as the Dharmas of Maitreya. Then in Penyul he studied Nagarjuna's collection of reasonings with Patsap Lotsawa.

He took vows and studied the vinaya with Geshe Sapukpa. Afterward he traveled to Takdur and practiced in the Kadampa tradition for five years. From Rachak Töntsul he heard teachings on the tantra of Hevajra, on Chakrasamvara, and on Mahamaya, and also on path and fruition as well as other instructions. From Drak Karwa, he received the hearing lineage of the Aro tradition of the Great Perfection.

When he was thirty, he met Master Gomtsul in the presence of Geshe Shawa Lingpa. Then he went to see Gampopa, but for nearly two months was not allowed to meet him. When he finally received permission, he offered ten white scarves and requested key instructions. Gampopa gave him a short teaching on path and fruition, saying, "I meditated on this and you should, too." Master Gomtsul served as Dusum Khyenpa's assistant, providing him with all his basic needs.

Then Dusum Khyenpa received empowerments from the Lord of Dharma Gampopa as well as key instructions on the path of method. He meditated on these for nine days, and great warmth arose. For the next nine months, he meditated wearing only a cotton cloth. Gampopa then told him, "You should go and meditate in Sangri." Rinpoche spent the three summer months there and said that his mind rested stably however he directed it and that his practice of insight was like the sun appearing from within the clouds. He went to pay his respects to his lama and then meditated for three years at Gampo. Undergoing extreme hardship, he became known as one of the toughest among the eight hundred meditators.

Gampopa then said, "Go to Ölkhar to meditate." When Dusum Khyenpa arrived at a cave on Ölkhar Driu Riwoche, a young woman appeared and said, "Don't stay here. My mistress is coming." Thinking that she was an ogress living in the cave, Rinpoche meditated on love and compassion. After he had practiced here for fourteen months, a special certainty arose in his mind, and many wondrous signs of the path appeared. Extremely happy, he went to offer his respects and discuss his experience with Gampopa, who was then at Jagö Retreat. After Dusum Khyenpa's report, Gampopa responded, "Alas! Khampa Gray Hair, I had great hopes in you, but you're quite mistaken. Now go back and continue with your meditation."

Dusum Khyenpa thought, "There's no mistake here," and six more months of meditation at Gampo produced nothing new. Then he returned to his lama: "Even if I meditated for one hundred years, that would not generate anything new in mind's essential nature. So even if I'm mistaken, I'm going to meditate like this."

Gampopa was delighted: "You have cut the ties to samsara." He then introduced Rinpoche directly to the depth of mind's abiding nature and gave him further key instructions to support his practice.

Afterward Jetsun Gampopa said, "Go to Dombu in the area of Tsang." Dusum Khyenpa went to Dombu, located in the lower part of Latö, where he met two brothers who were novice monks and disciples of Lama Milarepa. From them he heard teachings on *The Key to Mahamudra*. He received Dharma teachings from Shudön Moripa. Penpukpa gave him a Chakrasamvara empowerment and many key instructions from Jowo Je. From Gyapmo Yangkhangpa, he received explanations and key instructions on *The Two Books* of the Hevajra tantra. Then coming down to Jasang Rock in Penyul, he spent three summers and winters practicing in a sealed retreat. Innumerable qualities of the yoga of inner heat arose, and he composed a song in a blissful state of mind. He became known as the Lama of the Rock; in the way he appeared to others, he seemed to pass unhindered through mountains and boulders.

Then having gone to meet Gampopa, he spent nine months at Gampo. Again, the Jetsun advised him, "Go to Mön to meditate." So Dusum Khyenpa carried five *dre* of salt and traveled to see Garung, the king of Mön. One of the queen's female servants was a distant relative of Dusum Khyenpa and served as his translator. He met the king in person and was offered his support, so Rinpoche went to stay in the mountains of Mön.

Once, when he had run out of food, he was walking down the path to ask for more provisions when a tiger emerged from a forest. Dusum Khyenpa sat on top of a boulder while the tiger circumambulated it. Concluding that the tiger would not harm him, he continued along the path and met two young women who offered him two half gourds, each more than half full of liquor. Arriving at the king's palace, Dusum Khyenpa replenished his supplies. As he was returning up into the mountains, two people accompanied him to the place whence the tiger had come. While he was staying in the mountains again, he composed a song using the border between Tibet and Mön as an analogy.[3]

Later, as a parting gift, the king offered him several bolts of valuable cloth and a mantra against poison. On the return route, Rinpoche spent forty days with Lama Rechungpa and received teachings on establishing sessions and the six yogas. With ease, he passed through a discussion of Naropa's key instructions.

Afterward, he journeyed to Dakpo and met with Gampopa, who asked, "Did a tiger circumambulate you?"

"Yes, one did."

"That tiger was an emanation of a dakini. The two young women who offered you nectar were dakinis of a local protector, and they gave you siddhis."

Dusum Khyenpa remained a year at Dakpo, and then Gampopa said, "You should go to Gangkar." Once he arrived there, he stayed below Pabong Karlep, a retreat place of Master Padmasambhava. The dakinis offered Dusum Khyenpa nourishment while he passed the summer there engaged in the practice of extracting the essence. Many precious qualities arose in his mindstream. After the thought of his lama as the Buddha arose, Rinpoche sang a song about his own unworthiness. He said, "In general, if we lack devotion, positive qualities will not arise in our mindstream. I have never experienced a thought of my lama as ordinary."

That fall in Nyemo Nyidrung, he came down a ravine to a place near a fort. Close by was a house, and near it appeared four young women who were weaving. One of them said, "Master, are you asking for food?"

"Yes," he replied.

One of them went inside and said, "Come in!"

"Bring it out here," he requested.

"Nothing bad will happen. Do come in," she said. When he went inside, all four young women were present. They offered him food and drink in a half gourd resembling a skull cup. On the thumbs of the young woman who prepared the meal, he saw Chakrasamvara with four faces and twelve hands, embraced by his consort.

Among the food and drink they gave him was a stew of human fingers. Without hesitation, he consumed it all and found it to be extremely delicious. One of the young women then raised up to the sky a cup filled with a milky liquid. She offered it to him and he drank it. Afterward, just as he arrived at the door of the house, the four young women, weaving again, appeared outside near the gate of the fence that encircled the house. On the road leading down from this place, Dusum Khyenpa experienced the earth to be soft as a silk cushion, his body light as cotton, and his mind in a state of happiness free of identifying things as this or that. Later Gampopa would tell him that the four young women were the four dakinis of Chakrasamvara.

In a solitary retreat known as Dzong between Shu and Nye, Dusum Khyenpa met a woman meditator who was tending cattle. He asked her, "Who lives in that retreat up there?"

"My master stays there," she replied.

"Then I'd like to meet him."

"He's in retreat."

"I absolutely have to see him."

"I'll go ask my lama," she replied and left. Returning, she said, "Please go up."

When he entered the retreat, he found an older monk and nun. As he was prostrating, the lama made a sign that he should not, indicating the nun, but Dusum Khyenpa made excellent prostrations anyway.

When they had sat down for tea, Lama Dzongpa said, "Did four young women offer you a Dharma feast today?"

"They did."

"They were all dakinis. That substance in the stew was taken by the dakinis in Pamting, Nepal. It's from the corpse of the householder Ashoka's son Dharmasiddhi, which was being carried to the charnel ground of Tartita."

"Are the dakinis here now?"

"No, they're not. They went to the charnel ground of the Kashmiri city Sambhata. It is a place where the dakinis gather on the twenty-fifth of the black month, and they have traveled there for a feast. These dakinis bestowed siddhis on you. The two young women who offered you drink along the road in Mön were also dakinis."

Rinpoche thought, "This solitary retreat resembles my lama's Par Tsang retreat."

Lama Dzongpa asked, "Does this retreat resemble Par Tsang?" After that, Rinpoche did not dare think anything else. They conversed about many things.

The lama said, "Now you should do whatever your lama Gampopa says." Dusum Khyenpa said that he received from him "The Lightning-Strike Mahamudra" and many key instructions.

When Dusum Khyenpa went to Gampo to pay his respects, Gampopa said, "Drölgom and Khampa Gray Hair are both here," so that evening they had many delightful conversations.

Gampopa said, "Have you ever had a lama who knows things like that?"

"Yes, Lama Dzongpa does," Dusum Khyenpa replied. "He belongs to the third generation of Lama Naropa's disciples. He knew precisely what happened, how the dakinis had offered nourishment, and so forth. He explained everything to me. I didn't have to tell him."

Gampopa said, "When my lama Milarepa was resting in the samadhi of all-encompassing fire, I had to escape the flames. When he was resting in the samadhi of all-encompassing water, I saw him sitting on pooling water. He embodied the positive qualities that come from resting in the all-encompassing samadhis and also possessed extensive clairvoyance, yet he had not even an atom of conceit. In general, it is not correct for great meditators to be arrogant about their qualities. They should be kept hidden." So saying, he gave all the key instructions.

Dusum Khyenpa said, "Just as I was getting ready to go to Kampo Nenang, I had trouble with my leg and couldn't go." Gampopa had said, "You should go and this will benefit others."

"When I went to pay respects to Master Gomtsul in

Sangdum, he knew everything. I didn't have to speak. He told me."

Then, coming up from Gampo, he spent the three summer months at Lhari Gyenpo in Lower Shu. During that time he composed the song, "Ema! In the Charnel Ground of Aggregates."[4] He passed that winter at Shu in the Four-Sided Retreat. Later he related, "A young woman, who was a dakini, offered nourishment, but just a very small amount."

"Though I did not have plentiful food and clothing while practicing, I was never too slack or too strained in practice. Further, no one can make what's difficult easy the way I can. If at first you wish to be wealthy and cannot suffer the loss of food and clothing, your Dharma practice will not go well."

Around this time, he received many empowerments and blessings from Lama Bero, such as the Coemergent Chakrasamvara, Jetsunma Urgyenma, the spiritual songs of Telopa, and "The Coemergent Yoga of Inner Heat in Mahamudra." After Dusum Khyenpa had received the empowerment of glorious Chakrasamvara, he heard many key instructions.

Generally, Rinpoche remained in Central Tibet for thirty years: for ten of them, he listened to teachings and reflected upon them and for twelve, he practiced. Not once were his hands free of sweat. He stayed for eight years at Shu. Among his disciples were some forty deeply experienced practitioners and a great number of fortunate people whom he benefited as well. Dusum Khyenpa said, "Of all the things I received, I kept only what was needed at the time and gave the rest to my two lamas."

During this period, Master Gomtsul was staying at Lhalung with some three hundred monks. When Dusum Khyenpa was leaving for Eastern Tibet, he brought the gift of several reins for a horse as a parting gesture. The Master said, "Once I, too, was to go to Kampo Nenang, but a bad leg kept me from leaving. Since it's the lama's command, you should go one time. If you can't find food, or if the distractions become so great that the virtuous activity of your practice wanes, then come back here. I will die." At this, Dusum Khyenpa shed tears.

"Listen, let me tell you something," said Gomtsul. "I practiced in the past, and now I know all phenomena to be illusionlike. I can see Bodhgaya in an instant."

When Dusum Khyenpa was thinking about whether or not he should go to Drushi in Eastern Tibet, Dorje Paltsek of Kampo came to escort him. Rinpoche said, "The deity of Shu tried to stop me, but he could not prevent me from going."

Invited by the merchant Rinpal of Shigowa, Rinpoche went to Penyul, but he was not given the opportunity to go to Trewo. During this time, Lama Pakmo Drupa sent a message with the monk Yeshe Ö: "Do not depart for Eastern Tibet. Do not give too many initiations or perform a lot of consecrations. I fear there will be obstacles to your life."

"He cares a lot about me," Rinpoche said. "I can't say for sure whether I'll go to Shönnga Medrok or not. I won't give initiations or perform consecrations. I can live just as long as the lama Milarepa did."

Then he went back and stayed at the retreat of Tsurgyi Ngösang. The traveler Gotsun Yöndak of Költiwa invited him to Penyul but did not accompany him all the way to Trewo. When Dusum Khyenpa returned from Shu, he brought with him a fine horse and some other offerings and went to meet Master Gomtsul, who was staying at Nyingpo Seru.

Afterward he was invited to Trewo, so at the age of fifty, he departed for Eastern Tibet and stayed for two years at Kharser in Datö. He benefited some fortunate people and made offerings to Master Gomtsul. Then he went on to Trewo and lived there for two years, bringing benefit to some fortunate people. At the age of fifty-five, he went to Kampo Nenang, where he helped a large number of people, many of whom became great meditators and realized masters. Over five years Rinpoche offered fifty *dzo* and tea to this monastic seat.

At the age of sixty-seven, Dusum Khyenpa became ill. His attendants called all the monks together and said, "We're concerned that our lama is ready to depart from this world. What should we do?" The community of monks discussed this and decided that Lama Takdeuwa, about ten senior monks, plus all the others should perform long-life ceremonies, but these did not help. Then they thought that they should ask the lama to gather accumulations of merit. When they did, Rinpoche replied, "You think I'm going to die, but

I won't right now. I'll be able to live as long as Milarepa. Death will not come suddenly. And it would be all right to gather the accumulations." So he gave seven turquoise stones along with other offerings to the monastic seat and returned to good health.

Thinking that Dusum Khyenpa would depart for Central Tibet, Dorje Paltsek asked him to take medical treatment, and the whole Sangha echoed this request, so it was many years before Rinpoche could leave.

Geshe Tsultrim Chok from Kadrak sent two letters with a monk, saying, "Please do come to Tre and meet me. You're not allowed to say that you can't come." Around the same time, a wandering Chinese yogi traveled from India through Tönkun (in China) and up to Sakya. He said, "I've brought a letter from China. Please give it to the lama."

Dusum Khyenpa said, "I know what the Chinese letter means." When he was on the verge of leaving, he would not listen no matter how much the entire Sangha tried to postpone his departure for even a little while.

At the age of seventy-four, he traveled up the Yangtse valley, and in Beyul he established Geshe Gyang Kyawa and many others in well-being and happiness. For the summer, he stayed at Dongtra, where all the Sangha of Dridampa Chöchuk assembled, and he established them on the path that matures and liberates. Then he went to Tre, where he utterly pacified every disturbance so that all the people of the area became happy.

After Geshe Tsultrim Chok passed away, Rinpoche decided to stay on for two years and benefited many living beings.

He gave seven large turquoises and thirty containers of tea to the monastic center. Afterward, he stayed at Drilung Chebar. All the disciples gathered and about one thousand took ordination. He established many on the path of maturation and liberation. When Rinpoche went to Damey, he lived at Leu Karmar Monastery and matured all the disciples. He reconciled those in discord, liberated all the prisoners, and gave to the monastic center *The Prajnaparamita in One Hundred Thousand Verses* written in gold along with some turquoise and silver. In all these ways he benefited living beings.

Then Dusum Khyenpa left there and went to Central Tibet via the southern route. He offered the monastic seat four sets of *The Prajnaparamita in One Hundred Thousand Verses* written in gold and a volume of dharani mantras. In general, he offered one hundred ten texts written in gold, ten large turquoises, fifty dzo and horses, and many other objects. To the large monasteries in Central Tibet—mainly to Jowo Avalokiteshvara and Jowo Shakya—he offered seventy horses. Generally, he gathered the accumulation of merit by making more than one hundred great offerings.

Then he went to his seat at Tölung Tsurphu. He settled all the disputes at Tsalpa and Dakrawa and brought happiness to the people of the area. All the disciples from Central Tibet gathered there, and he matured and liberated them.

Chapter Twelve: Pure Visions

When Rinpoche first went to Gampo, he met Master Gomtsul in the presence of Shawa Lingpa and saw White Tara. If they had heard about this, the lamas of the past would have said that Gomtsul had attained stability in the creation phase.

When the Lord of Dharma Gampopa was conferring an empowerment, Rinpoche had a vision of Hevajra within a circle of light. When four Dharma friends were receiving an empowerment from Master Gomtsul, he appeared as the Heruka to each of them. When they asked about this, he replied, "The Heruka is me." Rinpoche had six clear visions of Master Gomtsul, three of Hevajra, and one of Vajra Yogini in a mass of light. When seeing Master Gomtsul as light, Rinpoche asked him about this and he replied, "I was meditating on the samadhi of all-encompassing water. I am also able to meditate on all the others."

When Dusum Khyenpa was at Drushi, he heard that the Lord of Dharma Gampopa's physical form had passed away, and so he left for Daklha. At Porok Dzongchung, he met Master Gomtsul and Master Pakpa. Clutching Lama Gomtsul's robes, Rinpoche shed tears. To pacify his torment, Gampopa, who had just passed away, suddenly and clearly manifested as a rainbow image, appearing in the same way to all three masters. They prostrated and at that moment the image faded away.

When Dusum Khyenpa was living at Nenang, Öchung Sangye traveled to Lhotö, begging along the way. He said, "I heard that the lama's monastic center at Daklha Gampo has been destroyed." Rinpoche looked into his own mind. First he saw Dakpo clearly, then Nepal, and finally, it was clear in all directions, filled with pure lands of the buddhas. Dusum

Khyenpa said, "It's not true that the monastic center was destroyed."

"How so?"

"I just looked and saw it," he replied.

At Nenang, after the memorial services of the Year of the Dog, he had a vision in the sky of innumerable gatherings of deities within their mandalas, including Shakyamuni and others. In particular, he saw Jetsun Yogini with one thousand heads and one thousand eyes, surrounded by thirty-six heroines. She said:

In the tantra of the Heruka:
The mind is said to be free of stains.
A pure emanation of Dharma
Has arisen in the form of Varahi.

At Nenang on the full moon of the first fall month, Dusum Khyenpa was performing ceremonies to commemorate Gampopa. When half a day had passed, there appeared numerous rainbows in the shape of parasols and mandalas, within which Gampopa and the attendants Lekdze and Drakdze were present as part of the principal deity's retinue. Gampopa said:

Son, the main point of the view is nonduality.
The main point of meditation is nondistraction.
The main point of conduct is union.
The main point of the result is the three undivided.

While Dusum Khyenpa was consecrating a statue of himself

and a statue of Hevajra along with his mandala, Rinpoche suddenly said during the recitation of the mantra of interdependence, "Chant 'The Praises of Tara.'" Afterward, when he was asked why he had done so, he replied, "Two Taras with eight deities each came and dissolved into the thangka."

The patron Kya Gönpawa requested that Dusum Khyenpa consecrate a shrine hall, and on the way there, Rinpoche had a vision of Paldenma. As he was performing the consecration, he heard in the sky the sounds of damarus and the Sanskrit ĀLI KĀLI. When he looked up, the sky was filled with immeasurable numbers of deities who had gathered. Rinpoche heard the words:

> View and meditation are like sky and water.
> Conduct cannot be negated or established.
> The natural state is the three inseparable.
> Like the sounds of lutes on a relative level,
> What they are and reality itself are inseparable.

In this region as well, he heard instructions on the bardo and on *The Praise to Hevajra in Eight Verses*. In Nenang, he had a vision of the Dharma protector Gönpo, who was standing above a great snow mountain in the midst of numberless curved knives swirling around in a dark black cloud.

When he was asked how many clear visions he had experienced in general, he replied, "I can't count how many I saw, but I have seen the thirty-five buddhas. There also appeared Marichi, Kali Kruddha Tara, the mandala of Hevajra, the mandala of Chakrasamvara, the mandala of Guhyasamaja,

Tranak and his assembly of deities, plus Yamantaka and his assembly of deities. During one feast offering, there appeared Mahamaya with her four deities, Jetsunma with her four deities, and Jetsunma Karpo as well. At Nenang appeared Achala and Nairatmya in union, Achala embraced by blue Tara, and Coemergent Hevajra. At Drushi, Coemergent Chakrasamvara appeared. At Sapuk, I had a vision of the mandala of Amrita Kundali with Nairatmya and eight deities. Further, on top of the mountain known as Palri in the south, I had a vision of naked Vajra Yogini experiencing bliss, with her hair flowing free. Without ornaments, she held a skull cup and curved knife while her right leg rested in the crook of her left elbow.

"Numerous letters of ĀLI KĀLI appeared in the sky. Then came a vision of Nairatmya and fourteen goddesses. I traveled through space to a charnel ground in Sri Lanka. I met Master Dorje Drilbupa, and my supplications were answered. After the memorial ceremonies for Gampopa, I went to the Grove of the Roaming Buffalo north of Bodhgaya. There I met Master Gomtsul, who said, 'Your ability to come here is amazing.' I received key instructions from him and we had many conversations."

Chapter Thirteen: His Dreams

At Gampo, Dusum Khyenpa saw in his dreams that all phenomena are like illusions and dreams. Then Gampopa said, "Transfer your consciousness to the pure land of Abhirati."[5] Dusum Khyenpa emanated into the sky as a mere illusion the mandala of Hevajra and eight deities. He also manifested himself as the central figure with eight deities and then dissolved them into the heart of those he had emanated into space. The eight deities, Chauri and so forth, said "Dza," and, withdrawing into Rinpoche, they faded from the sky. Gampopa was pleased and said, "We are in harmony."

In another dream, Dusum Khyenpa wished to see the Kashmiri city of Dripten and emanated a hundred and then a thousand bodies. Riding a swan and a lion throne, he traveled through space. When he arrived above Dripten, he heard waves of pleasant sounds that were unborn.

Once, he wished to see Tongkun, and on the way he arrived at Setsa Khar where Geshe Sherap had been born as the son of a rich lama. Rinpoche wondered, "Will he recognize me or not?" and he did, as he showed by smiling and being happy.

Again in a dream, Dusum Khyenpa experienced bliss as he sat on a stack of one hundred rocks. In front of him, eight dakinis clad in bone ornaments offered garlands of flowers. When he threw these blossoms into the sky, they transformed into a house of layered lotus flowers made of jewels. Emerging from this, he emanated a horse and a lion, and rode away on them.

As Dusum Khyenpa was traveling down the northern route, one night he dreamt that he found the plump corpse of a woman and cut it open. From the base of her ribs came numerous damarus, whose naturally arising sounds faded into space. Rinpoche departed together with these and arrived in the country of Uddiyana. A young woman said to him, "From here onward is the region of the wisdom dakinis and from here downward is the region of the worldly dakinis." He heard many key instructions that were a support for his practice.

At Drushi, he 'dreamt that a large serpent swallowed him whole except for his toes. At Pakri, he turned away lightning strikes with a threatening mudra. When Dza Rahula was in front of him at Kampo, Rinpoche turned him back just by thinking of him leaving. At Nenang, he dreamt that Gampopa was sitting beneath a rock overhang on a mountain in India. Meeting him, Dusum Khyenpa asked, "Lama, have you taken a miraculous birth?"

"No, I was born from the womb," he replied. Gampopa also gave him a Dharma teaching:

> Giving up your place of birth, you'll surely be free of desire and hatred.
> With real discipline, you'll surely go to the higher realms.
> Applying yourself to skillful means, you'll surely move along the path.
> Resting within the natural ground without altering, you'll surely realize the actual nature.

He also 'dreamt that an ascetic with a white body appeared and asked him, "Are you going to hear Dharma from the Buddha?"

Rinpoche thought, "Dipamkara has passed away and so

has the Buddha." So he asked, "Are you going to see Maitreya?"

"Yes."

A ray of sunlight appeared, and they rode it all the way to Tushita, where they found Maitreya in a sambhogakaya form teaching the Dharma to numerous white monks. Dusum Khyenpa heard this verse:

> In this, there's nothing to remove
> Nor anything at all to add.
> Looking authentically at the authentic
> And seeing authentically is liberation.

He gave many such teachings with profound meaning.

Rinpoche dreamt that he was departing to the west and saw in a tent of rainbow light Avalokiteshvara with eleven heads, who gave him a copious supply of medicine pills, saying, "Give all of these to others. They will bring benefit."

Dusum Khyenpa dreamt that he was Hevajra embraced by his consort and sitting on a lotus in a lake. In eight directions, the eight goddesses of Hevajra were playing lutes, and within their melodies came the invitation: "There is great bliss in the west." This was an omen of death, but it was averted and no harm occurred.

Once when he wished to travel to Nepal, the eight goddesses of Hevajra appeared and said, "It is not yet time for you to go." He said that even when he opened his eyes, they appeared in every direction.

At Nenang, during the full moon of the constellation Anuradha, he made offerings to his lama Gampopa. At the edge of night Dusum Khyenpa prayed to him, and during the pale light of predawn, he 'dreamt that Gampopa came and taught the Dharma. Rinpoche put this to song:

Yesterday on the Anuradha full moon,
I made offerings to the Three Jewels
To fulfill the guru's intentions.
In the evening I prayed to the guru;
At dawn in a dream as I slept,
I saw the guru come to me
And speak these words:

"Know view as awareness free of extremes.
Know meditation as the natural state free of change.
Know conduct as the four streams free of desire.
Know fruition as the three inseparable.
Know this as the dharmakaya, the benefit for oneself.

"Perform activity to benefit others:
Free of attachment, give generously.
Free of harming, maintain discipline.
Free of anger, cultivate patience.
Free of indolence, be diligent.
Free of distraction, meditate with concentration.
Free of elaboration, give rise to the wisdom of great bliss.
Dedicate these six for the benefit of others."

One night at Tsurphu he dreamt that he traveled to an Indian borderland. At the edge of the Kashmiri city of Surik, he met a master and his attendant. "Who are you?" he asked. "I'm Indrabodhi," was the reply. Rinpoche requested Dharma teachings, and Indrabodhi taught him the sadhana of Jetsunma Urgyenma. When he asked for another profound teaching, he was given the sadhana of Jetsunma with four heads and twelve hands along with all the associated practices. Later, in Dowo he had a vision of a female deity surrounded by thirty-six heroines with consorts. He asked the artist Gartön Horpo to make a painting of it.

In the Year of the Mouse, on the night of the third day of the dragon (or second) month, within a rainbow circle in the sky appeared a young woman, dressed in red and holding a red skull cup. She was adorned with the five ornaments and encircled by a retinue of four. She said, "Do not explain a single word of the profound meaning." Later, on the twentieth day at Shodrang, when he was blessing students by teaching the profound Dharma, these five young women, looking quite wrathful, appeared from among trees growing on a huge red rock.

"Who are you?" he asked.

"If you don't know who I am, I am Lekmi, royal consort of the king. Do not explain a single word of the profound meaning."

Later, on the evening of the the twenty-eighth, Dusum Khyenpa was giving teachings to the people of Kham. From among white clouds, the five young women appeared again with a fierce mien. Lekmi admonished him, "I said not to explain one word of the profound meaning and you did not listen!" Then all of them departed.

At Tsurphu, he had a dream on the night of the first day of the waxing moon in the serpent (or third) month of the Year of the Mouse. As soon as he looked to the southwest, he was on his way. In mid space the sound of thunder rumbled toward him. When he looked in that direction, within a mass of light, a yogi appeared wearing charnel-ground ornaments and holding a small drum in his right hand. "I am Maitripa," he said. "All the phenomena of samsara and nirvana can be included within two—the afflicted mind and the spontaneously present mind. Furthermore, the afflicted mind is included within the spontaneously present mind." Saying this, he faded away like a rainbow and vanished.

During the night of the twenty-third day of the serpent month, he 'dreamt that within a mass of light there appeared a yogi who held an arrow in his right hand and performed all activities with his left. He said:

> If you don't know who I am,
> I am known as Saraha.

When Dusum Khyenpa requested key instructions, Saraha said:

> If free of the four extremes, it is the view.
> If free of distraction, it is meditation.
> If free of refuting or proving, it is conduct.
> If free of abandoning or achieving, it is the result.

So saying, he dissolved like a rainbow and disappeared.

Again on the night of the twenty-seventh of this same

month, Dusum Khyenpa dreamt that he went to Daklha Gampo. There he held one end of a rainbow in his hands and, rolling it up, departed for Yangön in Getreng. Arriving there, he met Gampopa and described his previous dreams. His lama said, "You should understand all phenomena to be like dreams and illusions." As soon as these words were spoken, Dusum Khyenpa woke up.

Chapter Fourteen: Knowing How Others Have Left This Life for Another and Taken Rebirth

Rinpoche was asked in what worlds the lamas of the past had taken birth. He responded, "Lama Marpa has taken birth as a pandita in the city of Shrinagara near Palgyi Ri in the south. Sometimes appearing as a yogi, he is benefiting many living beings.

"Gampopa has taken birth as Shantivarman in the city of Padmini located in Karnawa between Kashmir and India. Sometimes he wears the robes of a fully ordained monk and sometimes he acts as a yogi. Through numerous types of conduct, he is benefiting living beings. Forty disciples have taken birth in that place.

"Gampopa has three emanations. The first emanation bears the name Drime Drakpa and benefits millions of living beings in the pure land called Placed in Bliss. The second emanation, named Bodhisattva Drime Dawa Drakpa, lives in the pure land known as Ornamented by Ten Million Pearls. He benefits King Drakpa Taye, his retinue, and many other living beings. The actual form of Gampopa has passed away from the city of Padmini. In the realm of the World of Infinite Thousands, he is famed as Ashoka.

"Master Gomtsul has been reborn to the west of India in one of the twenty-four sites, which is known as Kongka. Having converted a non-Buddhist king, he is benefiting many living beings. Master Sherap Jangchup lives at the base of Bird Foot Mountain. Ordained at eight, he is engaged in practice and benefiting many. Lama Penpuk took rebirth right in Tötsang and has the name Gaway Yeshe. Lama Palchenpo was reborn in the northern world into a realm called Ornamented by a Net of Pearls and has the name Palgyi Jungne Bepa. With the name Yeshe Jungne Drakpa, Master Trarawa was born in Sipri at the border of Chokro Dring. Master Sharawa Takdurwa was born in the city of Deden in Sepa at the very western end of the Rose Apple Continent. With the name Drakpa Taye, he is guiding millions of living beings.

"Master Patsap Lotsawa has taken birth on the far side of the Kashmiri city of Dripten. Called the Great Pandita Jungne Drakpa, he is maturing and liberating many living beings. Lama Dzongpa was born near the border of Kashmir and Nuche. He possesses the clairvoyances and practices with his previous consort to benefit many living beings. Master Chapa has taken the form of a pandita in the Kashmiri city of Dripten. Lama Ngulchuwa was reborn as the son of the Chinese king of Tongkun. In a dream, I met him on the Five-Peaked Mountain. Geshe Shudön Moriwa is teaching the Dharma through signs and benefiting many near Potala Mountain at the very western end of the Rose Apple Continent.

"Near the border of India and Nepal, Lama Rechungpa engages in a variety of conduct and has the name Ratnasukha. Master Sherap Dorje was born right in Penyul and practices in the Kadampa tradition. On the far side of Pamting in Nepal, Master Pakpa is a yogi with a consort and lives through begging. Abbot Sapukpa has taken birth as a pandita in the east of India and benefits many.

"On the far side of Nepal and the near side of India, on a rocky mountain there is a naturally arisen Palden Nakmo with sixty-four mamos. Master Padmasambhava sometimes came here thinking that if he did not come, the mamos would harm living beings."

Dusum Khyenpa also said, "Great yogis of the past, including the Great Brahmin Saraha, and lamas in the lineage, including Milarepa and Gampopa, all gathered together at the same time for a feast offering. I met them.

"I've seen bodhisattvas benefit others through an ordinary body.

"The practitioner from Gyal, Tre Chungpa, is the rebirth of Palpak Tsangpa. He has one rebirth in China and one in Nepal. The great king of Minyak is the rebirth of the yogi Matangki. His purpose was to help the king and to establish the people of this kingdom in virtuous activity. Further, as a powerful king, he could release many prisoners who would become his future disciples."

During the service to commemorate the anniversary of Gampopa's passing, Dusum Khyenpa saw that four students of Gampopa would create an immense benefit for beings and laughed.

Geshe Sherap Bum asked, "Why did you laugh?"

"Serkong Yeshe Nyingpo and Yasi Ngönmo will create immense benefit for living beings in the west. Gompa Shidze and Dakpo Sokgom will create immense benefit for living beings in the east.

"One novice monk who was Gampopa's disciple is also my oldest student. Now in a world to the south, he is connected with King Surabhibhadra and engaged in a bodhisattva's activity.

"Mönlam Lama, when you have passed away from here, you will be born to the east in Padmini. At this time, your abbot will be Ngaripa Sangpo, who has attained the level of a vidyadhara with power over his lifespan. Four lives previous to this one, he acted as your abbot in Padmini. Mönlam Lama, from the past up to now, you've taken rebirth and become a monk for five lifetimes without interruption."

When Rinpoche was staying at Drushi Retreat in Shu, a great meditator who was both a disciple and a patron passed away. Rinpoche commented, "Gompa Cha has been reborn in the area of lower Dzam, located in Dokham."

Later when Dusum Khyenpa went to this area of Dzam, many men and women came to pay homage to him. One boy, unafraid of the lama, picked up all the offerings and gave them to him. Rinpoche said, "This is the reincarnation of old Gompa Cha." Later, this boy along with a guide escaped from home and arrived at Nenang. Taking monk's vows and receiving key instructions, he became a great meditator, famous as the third rebirth of Dzam.

In the Male Year of the Hare, Rinpoche came up from Nenang to stay at Saktir, which was known as a hidden land. During this time, one of five monks died, and his friends asked Rinpoche where he was reborn. "He's been born in Tsang Rong as the son of Ratön Darmadrak." Eight years later in the Year of the Pig, when Dusum Khyenpa had already left for Central Tibet, a few monks traveled to Tsang. Begging along the way, they inquired about Ratön Darmadrak, and when they arrived in the town where he lived, they found that he did indeed have an eight-year-old son. The timing matched what Rinpoche had previously said, and all the villagers were amazed.

When he was staying at Sharwa, the younger brother of Changma Namkha Bar died. Dusum Khyenpa said, "He's been reborn in the Realm of the Thirty-Three Gods with the enjoyments of the gods and a stable shamatha practice."

Chapter Fifteen: His Appearing to Others

When Rinpoche was staying at Drushi and Ngösang, from his teeth came forth relics in a variety of shapes and colors: stupas, nets of vajras, *tsatsas*, and so forth. The relics could increase or decrease depending on the surrounding conditions. In particular, there arose the forms of Heruka, Yogini, and Khasarpani.

At Nenang, innumerable relics came from his teeth and upper arms. In the hidden land of Saktir, his eyes were not well, and when blood was let from a vein in his head, the vermilion liquid gave forth numberless relics. When he was at

Chebar in Drilung, two people carried away the soil from a place where he had urinated and strained it. One of them dreamt that there were relics in the dirt. When they shook it back and forth in water, four relics appeared. After Rinpoche heard this story, he said, "Bring those two people here." He gave them key instructions and their spiritual practice went well.

Further relics came from the middle of his forehead, his feet, and his saliva. Some supplicated him and relics arose; for others, relics appeared and then disappeared. Those with pure perception had pure visions. Dusum Khyenpa manifested in a variety of ways in order to clear away doubts.

At Kampo Nenang, while two geshes and a few monks were performing the rituals of an empowerment, one of the geshes saw Dusum Khyenpa as Vajra Yogini and related this to his friends. When Dzamtön Sangye was participating in a feast offering, he saw Rinpoche as Heruka Chakrasamvara. During the memorial ceremonies for Gampopa, a great meditator from Central Tibet saw Avalokiteshvara, yellow in color with one thousand arms and one thousand eyes, in the place where Rinpoche was sitting at the head of the monks. The meditator prostrated to him until daybreak, which brought the meditator great merit, and he became famous as Lama Samye Bardrak.

At Sopuk in Dzamyul, while a monk from Dzam was receiving key instructions from Rinpoche, he appeared to the monk as the Jowo Avalokiteshvara. This deity taught him the practice up to the full visualization of Avalokiteshvara and the transmission of the mantra. The monk gained faith and meditated, becoming famous as Dzane Gomsang.

During the full moon of the first month of autumn, when memorial services for Gampopa were being performed at this same monastery, Dusum Khyenpa appeared to a senior monk as the Bhagavan Shakyamuni, sitting on a lion throne and teaching.

In Lungmeda, while the monks of Tsachilpa were performing the rituals of an empowerment they were to receive, Lama Lha saw Dusum Khyenpa as Vajradhara. Two nights later, he saw him as Vajra Yogini, and three nights later, he appeared as Jetsun Telopa.

When Dusum Khyenpa went to Datö Kharsa, all the leaders of Datö assembled there. At that time, he had been asked to perform a consecration in Kharsa. When they were reciting the mantra of interdependence, the images of Rinpoche and Shakyamuni appeared in the vase section of the large reliquary stupa. They manifested in the same way to all who had gathered, which amazed everyone. In particular, faith arose in Chambu Pönring, who then meditated and developed experience and realization. He made an offering of fourteen hundred kilos of barley (instead of the traditional roasted barley along with butter).

At Tsurphu Monastery while Tsangpa Tsulseng was receiving an empowerment, Rinpoche appeared to him as Hevajra with eight heads and sixteen arms. Light rays shone from the deity's heart and bestowed the empowerment by entering into a monk who was present. Afterward, Hevajra kept appearing until Tsangpa Tsulseng fell asleep.

At Chebar in Drilung, Rinpoche was sitting at the head of a large number of the Sangha. A tantric practitioner wanted to make prostrations, but he did not see Dusum Khyenpa. The attendants all pointed him out, but the practitioner still could not see him. Jowo Jangchup also pointed to Dusum Khyenpa, but even so the practitioner did not see Rinpoche. Jowo Jangchup was deeply saddened and tears came to his eyes. The Sangha and patrons were all astonished.

Wanting to offer prostrations, Karma Denma went to Yangön, but he did not see Rinpoche; instead, he saw a white stupa in the place where Rinpoche usually sat. Karma Denma turned around and left.

At Sado, a Kadampa called Drodo Töntsun came to offer prostrations and a tiger pelt to Dusum Khyenpa, but he did not see Rinpoche. All his companions prostrated and inquired after Dusum Khyenpa's health, but Drodo Töntsun still did not perceive him. Only after a long while was he finally able to see him.

While Dusum Khyenpa was staying at Nenang, he appeared barefoot to Dzamtön Sangye, who was staying in his retreat about four days' travel to the east of Nenang. When Dzamtön Sangye went to offer prostrations and inquire after his health, Rinpoche vanished while a seat was being prepared for him.

In a faraway place, a disciple suffering from the torments of an illness supplicated his lama, and Dusum Khyenpa came to give him a blessing. The pain of the illness subsided and at that very moment, Rinpoche disappeared.

When Dusum Khyenpa was staying near Dongnga in Drilung, he appeared to the great practitioner Wenpa, who had supplicated him from his place in Tre called Raktay Sa. Rinpoche gave him Dharma teachings and then, fading like a rainbow, vanished.

While Dusum Khyenpa was staying at Tsurphu Monastery, the great practitioner Trewo Gomchen was suffering terribly from an illness. The very moment he supplicated Dusum Khyenpa, Rinpoche appeared in order to give him an empowerment with his foot. As Trewo Gomchen began to prostrate, Rinpoche said, "There's no need to prostrate. The obstacle of this sickness will not come to you." Dissolving like a rainbow, he disappeared.

Geshe Sumpa saw Dusum Khyenpa as Hevajra. Master Ratön saw him as five changing lights. While receiving the blessings of Shal Chikma, Master Sangye saw him sitting in space with light radiating from his face. Later, even after Dusum Khyenpa had passed away, Master Sangye saw his face again and again.

For the benefit of living beings, Rinpoche went from Eastern to Central Tibet. One day in the (first) summer month of Rawa in the Year of the Bird, when he was residing at Lhalung near Tsurphu Monastery, Dusum Khyenpa said, "Last night I 'dreamt that I went to an Indian charnel ground where several Indian yogis had gathered to practice together."

Around the same time, in the temple of Tangchu in Western Tibet, a Dharma teacher from the area was sewing robes. Three wandering yogis wearing only cotton and carrying skull cups in their hands appeared to him along with a barefoot yogi who was about sixty years old and dressed only in cotton cloth. Wearing conch-shell earrings, this Tibetan carried a skull cup and a cane made of wood with metal caps on either end. The Tibetan yogi and the teacher engaged in a long conversation. "Where did you come from?" asked the teacher.

"On the way here, I came from Bodhgaya through Kashmir and Surapa."

"Why did you go to India?"

"I went for a great ceremony in Bodhgaya," the Tibetan yogi replied.

"Well, I heard that many realized masters came to the great ceremony for the Year of the Bird. Did you meet any of them?"

"I heard something like that too," the yogi said. "At that time, in the city of Jalandhara in southern India, the king Dawa Nampar Nönpa was celebrating a feast offering at the charnel ground of Hahadrok. He supplicated yogis who were realized masters and who possessed the clairvoyances and the ability to perform miracles. Four came from southern India. The great accomplished master Mitra Jogi said that there were also two from Tibet, for a total of six."

"Who were the accomplished masters from India and Tibet?" the teacher asked.

"The four from India were Indrabodhi, Jalandhara, Krishnacharya, and Shingpopa, and the two from Tibet were Dharmakirti and Dharmashila.

"What are these two like?"

"Dharmashila, or Chökyi Tsultrim, has the instructions on achieving immortality. He resides in western Ngari, where he is benefiting others by building a temple. Shri

Dharmakirti, or Chökyi Drakpa, has the key instructions on the sufficient and decisive path of mahamudra that is based on the paths of the channels and winds. He lives in the lower part of Tibet. It seems that he is famed as Lama Gray Hair.[6] We are going there."

The teacher said, "Lama Gray Hair is very famous. I was also thinking of going there, but I heard that he would not stay long in this world and soon depart for another place. I doubted I could hear a complete Dharma teaching, so I couldn't make up my mind. I made no plans to go but was not comfortable staying either."

The yogi replied, "Haven't you seen *The Prayer for Excellent Conduct*?

> For the sake of one disciple
> The Buddha remains for an aeon
> And also swiftly brings that person to maturity,
> Just like a seedling given warmth and moisture.

"If others supplicate for the benefit of living beings," he explained, "the buddhas will remain for aeons. Never part from faith and devotion. Go quickly now to the lama. You'll receive the entire teaching for sure."

At this the teacher felt a special joy and asked for key instructions. The Tibetan yogi stood up and went over to the wandering yogi, who was covered in ashes. From nearby him, he fetched a text written on rolled-up birch paper. Referring to this, the Tibetan yogi gave the teacher explanations, and a special faith arose in him. Then the yogi gave the text to the teacher, saying, "This text, 'The Four Aspects

That Can Free the Mindstream and Bring Forth Blessings and Power,' is a very profound key instruction. Keep it for yourself and do not show it to others. Later you will meet me again." So saying, he placed a firm seal of secrecy on the teachings.

The teacher returned to his house. He wanted to invite the yogis to a Dharma feast later the next morning. When the teacher went to find them, the caretaker of the temple said, "The yogis left just after you did." Though people were sent everywhere to ask if anyone had seen or heard of them, the answer was always no. Then a special certainty arose within the teacher, and he made ready to go from Central Tibet to see Lama Gray Hair.

In the middle summer month of the Dog Year, the teacher went to the monastery of Tölung Tsurphu. There he received from Dusum Khyenpa empowerments, blessings, and key instructions. Afterward, he spent the summer practicing in retreat. In the fall, Dusum Khyenpa gave a brief account of what had happened before to a few of the monks so they knew something about it.

The teacher had the thought to ask if the four yogis from before had come to Tsurphu, but Dusum Khyenpa said, "You can ask that tomorrow morning," so he did not dare to question further.

Then the teacher from Tsang thought, "I should get rid of these doubts once and for all," so he arranged all the articles for a ceremony in the house of a monk from Kham, Pön Drakseng. The teacher invited Dusum Khyenpa and gathered about ten of the oldest monks, including Lama Takdeuwa, Geshe Könchok Senge, and Gompa Tsultrim

Gyalpo. During the ceremony, the teacher fervently supplicated Rinpoche to tell about the previous encounters. As if pointing to an actual event with his finger, Dusum Khyenpa spoke of them clearly and in accordance with the teacher's own experience. All were astonished.

The teacher asked, "Who were the three wandering mendicants?"

Rinpoche replied, "The second Indrabodhi, Shinglopa, and Krishnacharya. I was the one who gave you the key instruction, which I had received from Indrabodhi. It is called 'The Four Aspects That Can Free the Mindstream and Bring Forth Blessings and Power.' Krishnacharya was the vajra master of the Indian feast in the charnel ground. You have been my disciple for four lifetimes, so this is the fifth time we have met. I came to cut through your doubts and get you to meditate. It is excellent that you studied and explained Dharma; however, this was tarnished by the eight worldly concerns. It is good that you came to meditate. If we hadn't met this time, you would have gone along with merely your studies and explanations."

Lama Takdeuwa asked, "How did you meet in these four previous lives?"

Dusum Khyenpa replied, "Previously in India, the teacher was born as the smith Ratnashri and generated bodhichitta as my disciple. Afterward, when he was born to the north of this continent in Rewa, I was his abbot. Then when he took birth as Metok Sherap Sangpo on the continent of Superior Body, I gave him the key instructions of 'Prajna: The Sessions of Six Dharmas.' The life before this one, he was born as the Brahmin Gyalwa Sherap in a remote area of India on the shore of an ocean. I gave him all four empowerments. Knowledgeable about treatises, he acquired the imprints for meditation, and therefore it was easy for him to develop certainty in view and meditation.

Lama Takdeuwa asked, "Jetsun, you have many emanations that are benefiting living beings. These days, how many are there in the world?"

"It's not certain," replied Dusum Khyenpa, "but it seems that there are four who are benefiting living beings. The first one, Bhikshu Geway Lodrö, lives on the far side of Ngari and this side of Kashmir in a city called Surik. A previous disciple named Den Chung died and was born here. For his sake, Geway Lodrö built a place for Dharma, and he also benefits many other living beings.

"The second one lives in the the monastery of Lama Bero, located in Lande on the border of Tibet and Nepal. He has taken birth as Genyen Chökyi Drakpa and benefits beings by teaching the Dharma through signs.

"The third one is a yogi who lives in the south of India. To those with pure vision, he appears as Avalokiteshvara, and others call him Avalokiteshvara. He does not stay in a fixed place.

"The fourth lives in a realm of the world to the east as a realized master who appears as the king Drakpa Taye. If he were not its king, he would not be able to tame the kingdom, so he has chosen this way to benefit many living beings. There are countless others similar to these four."

If people supplicate these emanations, they will come no matter how near or far, for they are innumerable.

When Dusum Khyenpa was staying at Kampo Nenang, the leader and patron Gönpawa invited him to consecrate a temple. During this time, it appeared to Pön Gomdor, the temple's manager, that when Rinpoche was reciting the mantra of interdependence and offering grains of barley visualized as flowers, these blossoms naturally offered themselves and descended on all the objects of worship. When he told this to others, everyone was amazed.

Three days' journey to the south of Nenang, Rinpoche was invited to perform a consecration by the great yogi Geshe Shakya, a disciple of the Nepali Ḣamngu Karpo and a second-generation disciple of Naropa. During this consecration, the men and women who were far away saw the temple blazing with fire; for those nearby, the fire was circling round the temple; and for the patrons and others who were inside, all the objects of worship moved and made sounds. A large cast-metal statue of Vajrasattva held his emblem, a vajra, poised on the end of his right ring finger, but this vajra had been crooked from the time it was cast. No one else could find a way to straighten it, but Rinpoche was successful. Everyone found this wondrous.

Monge Geshe Josey invited Dusum Khyenpa to perform a consecration at Khakar in Jamyul, a four-day journey east from Nenang. During the recitation of the mantra of interdependence, it appeared to the geshe that the flowers on the mandalas were bobbing up and down just like the grains in boiling water. Then the flowers flew up and fell onto the objects of worship. Everyone saw this and was amazed. The geshe lauded Rinpoche with twenty verses of praise, in which he wove together references to the paths and levels as they relate to the paramitas.

Many others saw wondrous things. Flowers offered themselves and alighted on the objects of worship, which also moved, radiated lights, and gave off sounds. The crippled, the bent, and others with ailments got better when he slapped them. When the mute were given key instructions, they could speak. Likewise, for those struck by the mischief of *mimayin* spirits,[7] he offered a torma and spoke the truth, which brought benefit. In these ways, he helped the afflicted. By his transforming the perception of those who clung to the reality of things they could give up the activities of this life and enter an authentic path. These practitioners were so numerous as to be immeasurable, beyond words.

Dusum Khyenpa was asked, "You have consecrated hundreds of objects of worship that were possessed by ghosts. You have given empowerments to hundreds who suffered from leprosy or had broken samaya. How is it that you have not been defiled by all these?"

Rinpoche replied, "When a yogi's mind does not perceive in terms of dualities and he has realized that all phenomena in their vast array have the same taste, he then abides without interruption in the natural state. For such a yogi, neither contamination as an entity nor objects that produce contamination exist."

After he had stayed at Tsurphu Monastery for five years, on the full-moon day in the seventh month of the Year of the Mouse, Dusum Khyenpa performed the memorial services for Gampopa. At that time, in order to gather the accumulation of merit, he offered to the main seat of Dakpo eighteen volumes written in gold and twelve volumes of blank pages (thirty volumes in all), plus a kilo and a half of red-veined turquoise famous throughout the world and many other precious objects. In general, he gave one hundred volumes of scriptures and many different kinds of wealth to all the monasteries.

Dusum Khyenpa said, "When the monks assemble to conduct ceremonies, it requires a great deal of work, and so you should not continue to do them. If you want to go to Eastern Tibet or someplace to meditate or to study, go wherever you wish—Eastern Tibet, Daklha Monastery, or the border of Tibet and Mön." Some said he would go to Eastern Tibet and some thought he would definitely go to Gampopa's main seat. All had their doubts.

For three months, significant omens continuously appeared—rainbows in the sky, earthquakes, and roaring sounds. His attendants and the senior monks said, "When Rinpoche was not feeling well at Nenang, he stated that he would live as long as Milarepa. That would be eighty-three or eighty-four years. Now he has come to that age and we're worried that he might depart." When Rinpoche turned eighty-four, in the New Year of the Ox on the third day of the tiger (or first) month, he withdrew the mandala of his nirmanakaya form and departed for the realm of Khechari.

At Tsurphu, on the tenth day during the cremation, many different appearances were seen. All who were present had a similar experience of the sun staying in the sky twice as long as usual. Some people saw thirteen, eight, or seven suns. These also coalesced and separated. The sun's rays appeared in the shape of a parasol fashioned of peacock feathers. Dakas and dakinis wearing bone ornaments filled the entire sky. A rain of flowers fell. Rainbow parasols floated in tiers above his body. The fire gave off sounds in a variety of lovely tones that could not be identified. The smoke turned into rainbows, and Dusum Khyenpa could be seen in their midst. Flights of birds circled around the rising smoke. Flocks of vultures, herds of wild animals, and other miraculous sights appeared to people. Those not engaged in spiritual activity became engaged. All those already engaged developed their practice further. For the great meditators, wondrous samadhis arose.

What remained after the cremation was his heart, which was full of love for living beings, his tongue, which had taught the genuine Dharma, and relics, which came from his perfection of both kinds of bodhichitta. Based on his stable practice of the creation stage, images of the deities and others came forth, and a small amount was given to each of the close disciples. At the glorious Tsurphu Dowo Monastery, representations of his body were created for the benefit of others; a great room for the relics was constructed; and a golden stupa in the style of the Glorious Drepung Stupa was built. It naturally consecrated itself and gave forth blessings that reached the limits of space.

Chapter Sixteen: Incarnations in India

Rinpoche was asked, "After this life, what incarnations will you take?"

"To the west of India, twelve days' journey to the northwest of Uddiyana in a city called Kartika, I will be born to my father Dharmasiddhi and mother, Mahaprajna, as a yogi called Prajnashila. Gampopa will take a birth from a womb in the city of Padmini and have the name of Shantivarman. In this city, a debate will occur between the Lord of Dharma Gampopa, who will be the one holding a thesis, and a non-Buddhist pandita, who will seek to disprove it. Lama Rinpoche will be the winner, so the non-Buddhist teacher will become Buddhist and receive the name Dharmaraja. The name of the non-Buddhist king will be Mahajina. In the city of Kartika, there will live a pandita called Bodhivajra who will have many good qualities.

"Among Gampopa, Bhikshu Gomra, Shidze, Gartön, Serkong Yeshe Nyingpo, Somshi Yeshe Nyingpo, Yasi Ngönmo, Gyache, Gyachung, Drakdze, Nyakde Tönpa, Rokgom, and Yönten Nyingpo—six will be able to engage in the yogic conduct of awareness.

"Gampopa will convert a non-Buddhist king through nonconceptual meditation and at the same time, the pandita will convert the king of Kartika. Lama Rinpoche, the Buddhist pandita, and a non-Buddhist pandita will all be supported by the king. Between the cities of Padmini and Kartika there will be very few cities. The whole area will not be Buddhist, but everyone will convert to Buddhism. It will take about two days to travel between the two cities.

"I will meet Gampopa again. Here, the patron Gönpawa

will be born as the son of a minister and take ordination. Some of you will also take birth in the city of Karnapa. Seven of you—Yönten Ö, Gendun Ö, Mönlam Lama, Yeshe Ö, Tönpa Tsulseng, Gendun Drak, and you—will all be born simultaneously into the merchant caste. These three cities are found together in one area.

"Furthermore, Master Rinchen Gyaltsen, Tönpa Sangye, Tönpa Changdrak, Tönpa Sö, Pön Dharmaraja, Shakya Sherap, Gomngön, Dorje Bum, Geshe Rinchen Drak, Wangchuk Drak, Öser Lama, Yönten Lama, Darma Senge, Dorje Tsöndru, Jangpa Lhasowa, and others will also be born in this territory. Many of you will meet Gampopa numerous times. If you haven't done so yet, you will in the future lives."

Chapter Seventeen: His Birth in Lhodrak

Dusum Khyenpa was asked, "After India, where will you be born?"

"I will take birth in Central Tibet in seven places of practice in Lhodrak," he said. "It will be a birth for the benefit of one disciple and I will not stay long. I will meet some of you there."

Chapter Eighteen: His Birth in a Realm of the World to the East

Rinpoche was asked, "And where will you be born after that?"

"At Urupa in southern India, I will be born in a place of

the dakinis called Kongka. In that area, there is a city called Patala where the patron Gönpawa will take birth as a king and stay on an authentic path. You will meet me there. Afterward, for many lives to come, you will not need me. Many other living beings will be benefitted."

Just as a wish-fulfilling jewel creates a variety of emanations Dusum Khyenpa will benefit living beings until the karma of each one is exhausted. One could never finish speaking or writing about his lives.

> This *Golden Isle*, the life story of a great bodhisattva,
> You should treasure and respect, never ceasing to look at it.
> As my mind is small, I request patience for any contradictions.
> By this virtue, may all become disciples of the Lord of Dharma.

This account is called The Golden Isle: The Precious Lives of the Lord of Dharma in Eighteen Chapters. *It gathers several accounts of the lama and his disciples. Taking these reports to be valid, Galo wrote this account as an ornament for Tsurphu Dowo Monastery.*

A Strand of Pearls

Composed by Lord Dusum Khyenpa

A Ritual of Going for Refuge and Rousing Bodhichitta

He has fully trained in supreme bodhichitta
And perfected the two accumulations.
Endowed with two wisdoms, he has gained the result,
 the three kayas.
He has no clinging and shines the sunlight of
 compassion for others' sake:
I bow with respect to my precious lama.

Now we have attained a human body with the perfect leisures and resources and entered the gate of the Buddha's teachings. In order to practice Dharma, it is critical to first meditate on death and impermanence. In Atisha's words:

Always reflect on death; assess the karma you have
 accumulated;
Offer to the Three Jewels; meditate on the nondual
 nature.

First, it is extremely important to meditate on death and impermanence. Things are said to be impermanent in the same way as a stream on a steep mountainside, a lamp flickering in a strong wind, water bubbles, or a bird feather blown by the wind.

There are two types of impermanence: external impermanence and internal impermanence. External impermanence is like the change and progression of the seasons through spring, summer, autumn, and winter.

There are two types of internal impermanence: the impermanence of the continuum and momentary impermanence. The impermanence of the continuum is that first our mothers give birth to us and we are little babies. Then we are small children, and then we are in the prime of life. In the end, we get old and reach death. Momentary impermanence is all the moments that have passed since we have gathered here for this empowerment.

If we could add to our lives when they were over, we would look into it. But there is no extending life. When it is done, there is nothing other than death. As Master Shantideva says:

> Never staying, day or night,
> This life is always dwindling.
> If life is never getting longer,
> Why would one like me not die?

Whatever we do, there is nothing other than death. At that time, possessions, friends, and relatives cannot accompany us. In Master Shantideva's words:

> Even the flesh and bones we're born with
> Will fall apart and scatter about.
> What need to speak of friends and others?

Even the flesh and bones we are born with will not go with us. What does go with us is the Dharma. From *The Sutra of Advice to the King*:

> When the time approaches, the king will die;
> His wealth and friends and relatives will not follow him.
> Wherever a person is born, wherever they go,
> Karma will follow them like a shadow.

Just as the shadow of a bird flying in the sky moves over the earth and arrives wherever the bird lands, whatever virtuous or unvirtuous acts you have done will follow you, and their results will ripen all of a sudden. This is why it is said that nothing other than Dharma will help at the time of death.

When you die, you do not become nothing. There is rebirth. You take a body due to the power of karma. If you have performed the ten misdeeds motivated by the three poisons, the result is rebirth in the lower realms. The suffering is long lasting, severe, and difficult to bear. If you perform the cause, the ten misdeeds motivated by hatred, you will be reborn in the hells. There are the eight hot hells, the eight cold hells, the occasional hells, and the sixteen surrounding hells, in all of which there is unfathomable suffering. If you perform the cause, the ten misdeeds motivated by greed, the result is to be reborn as a hungry ghost. The hungry ghosts have external obscurations, internal obscurations, specific obscurations, the obscurations of hunger and thirst, and innumerable other sufferings. If you perform the cause, the ten misdeeds motivated by the affliction delusion, the result is to be reborn as an animal. Although there are in general thirty-six different kinds of animals, they may be summarized as two: those that live in the depths and those scattered about. The depths of all the outer oceans are teeming with living beings the size of the dregs from brewing beer. They have innumerable sufferings such as the larger eating the smaller and killing each other. It is said that when one of them is eaten, the ocean becomes red with its blood.

Now, the animals in human lands are in animal heaven. But the birds in the sky have the fear of being killed by others and so forth, which is as painful as being struck by one hundred spears. All those domesticated by humans experience innumerable sufferings, such as being burdened with loads they cannot carry, being forced to pull a plow although unable, being castrated, having their noses pierced, being slaughtered, and so forth. Master Shantideva said:

> It would be right for me to think
> All day and all night only this:
> Nonvirtue leads to suffering—
> How can I free myself from it?

When you contemplate death and impermanence; karma, cause, and effect; and the suffering of the lower realms, that creates the wish for the higher realms and happy states. This alone, it is said, is enough to eliminate rebirth in the lower realms.

In addition, performing the ten virtues that are not the path[8] brings rebirth in the three higher realms, but there are no friends or happiness for those born there. They enjoy the causes of suffering while seated on the edge of the precipice to the lower realms. Even those born as gods will die and fall to lower realms. Gods leave goddesses. Goddesses leave gods.

These and innumerable other sufferings are as painful as the suffering of a camel mare losing her calf or of a fish tossed onto hot sand.

If you are born as a demigod as well, you experience innumerable sufferings of perpetual strife and fighting. Jewel mountains are hurled back and forth. There is anger, fighting, hatred, jealousy, killing, injury, and untold sufferings that are no different from those in the reviving hell.[9]

If you are born as a human, there are the three or eight sufferings. First are the four primary sufferings—the four great rivers of birth, aging, sickness, and death. In the suffering of birth, there is the pain of being in the mother's womb. If the mother eats her fill, there is pain as if you were being squashed by a mountain. When the mother is hungry, there is as much pain as if you were being strung up and dangled. The pain of birth is as great as being squeezed between great mountains or getting flayed. Touching the ground is like falling into a pile of hot coals or a bramble of thorns. There are also innumerable other sufferings.

Then when you get old, your hair turns gray, your teeth fall out, your eyes get cloudy, and you go deaf. Your back gets bent. Standing up is like pulling. Sitting down is like falling. Your feet cannot support your body, and there are many other sufferings as well.

Regarding the suffering of illness, if there is no way to bear the pain of a toothache now, what need to speak of the sufferings of other illnesses?

Regarding the suffering of death, at the time of death, you lie on your deathbed and take your last nourishment, a single drop of water. Those close to you surround you, but only you will experience the pain of this life ending. When the visions of yakshas appear, you expel feces and urine as if shooting an arrow. Your friends and relatives can do nothing. Food and wealth do not help the dying. As Master Shantideva said:

> Although my friends and family,
> Surround me as I lie on my bed,
> Only I alone will feel
> The pain of my life being cut.
>
> When Yama's henchmen have me seized,
> What help are family and friends?
> Only merit could save me then,
> But that I have not cultivated.

The suffering of death is unbearable.

There are many other sufferings: the suffering of not being able to maintain and protect what you have; the suffering of not getting what you do not have, even though you look for it; the anxiety of meeting your hateful enemies; and the anxiety of separation from your loved ones. There is anxiety over not having a son; anxiety over not having a daughter; anxiety over the decline of your country or faction, your good name and fame. These and other sufferings are immeasurable. As it is said:

> Those in samsara have no joy;
> Feces has no pleasant scent.

When you meditate on the defects of the three realms of sam

sara, you feel like a person thrown into a prison who does not want to stay there for even an instant, thinking, "When will I be free? How can I get out of here?" Similarly, the nature of the three realms of samsara is suffering. There is not an instant of happiness that is not suffering, and so you begin to think, "How can I free myself from the great ocean of suffering that is the three realms of samsara?" Then the wish for your own peace and nirvana will come. That is enough to eliminate remaining in the three realms of samsara. Although you might free yourself alone from samsara, you would have no friends or happiness.

Among all the sentient beings of the three realms, there is not one who has not been your father or mother. From *The Sutra of Beginningless and Endless Samsara*:

> Though you might make the earth into balls
> The size of juniper berries,
> They would not equal the number of your mothers.

You could take this huge earth and make it all into balls the size of medium peas, using it all up, but they still would not approach the number of times that any single sentient being has been our parent. Therefore, only mothers are kind. The food they have given us equals Mount Meru. The cloth they have clothed us in equals the southern clouds.

> We have drunk more milk from her breast
> Than there is water in the four oceans.

Thus only mothers are very kind. They do not use for themselves the food, drink, clothes, and other things they treasure, but instead give them all to their child. They lie on the wet ground themselves and lay their child on the dry. They hold their baby to their bodies' warmth. They clean off filth with their own mouths. They do not let their child out of their sight. They always think, "Wouldn't it be great if my child alone had the best and turned out better than anyone else in the world?" Thus only mothers are kind.

Since our mothers have been so very kind, we need to repay them with gratitude. When we look to see whether our mothers are happy or not, according to the scriptures, our mothers in hell have the suffering of heat and cold and being cooked and burnt. Our hungry-ghost mothers have the suffering of hunger and thirst. Our animal mothers suffer from stupidity and delusion. Our demigod mothers have the suffering of conflict and strife; our god mothers the suffering of death and falling to lower realms; and human mothers have the sufferings of busyness, destitution, and so forth. Our mothers do not have a single instant of happiness that is not suffering.

Now develop the resolve that you will achieve omniscient buddhahood for the sake of your mothers and that you will liberate them from the ocean of samsara's suffering and bring them to unexcelled enlightenment. That is enough to prevent us from remaining in lower vehicles, it is said.

Then you must meet a genuine lama who gives you true spiritual advice. They point out that all the phenomena of samsara and nirvana are your own mind so you realize that the nature of your own mind is emptiness free of all elaborations and that samsara and nirvana are nondual and the same in essence. Never varying from that state eliminates clinging to things and attributes.

What precedes all of that is going for refuge to the Three Jewels. In the abhidharma:

> Everyone may take vows, of course,
> But only after going for refuge.

You must go for refuge in order to take the vows of individual liberation. You must go for refuge in order to take the bodhisattva vows, too. You must go for refuge to receive an empowerment of the secret mantra as well.

This present occasion is an empowerment of the secret mantra. There are four classes of secret mantra: the action tantra, conduct tantra, yoga tantra, and unexcelled yoga tantra. Among those, this is the unexcelled tantra, of which there are two sections: the unexcelled father tantras and the unexcelled mother tantras. This is from an unexcelled mother tantra, the profound and exalted tantra of Chakrasamvara. Within that tantra, this is the bestowal of empowerment and blessings by way of Vajra Yogini, the mother who gives birth to all the buddhas of the three times. This must be preceded by refuge and bodhichitta, which is why they are taught.

I prostrate to the genuine lamas. It is the Three Jewels that protect us from all the suffering of samsara. Since there is no one else who can protect us, think that innumerable buddhas and bodhisattvas are present in the sky before you. Think that you will abandon samsara, this ocean of suffering, and achieve unexcelled, precious enlightenment. This is the purpose for which you go to the Three Jewels for refuge. Then repeat after the master:

"Master, please consider me. From this time onward as long as I live, I, named (*name*), go for refuge to the supreme among those with two feet, the Buddha. I go for refuge to the supreme among freedoms from desire, the Dharma. I go for refuge to the supreme among all communities, the Sangha." Recite this three times.

Then the master says, "This is the method," and the students reply, "It is excellent."

Merely going for refuge is not enough; we also must train in the precepts. First there are the three distinguishing precepts, whose purpose is to distinguish ourselves as superior to ordinary beings and non-Buddhists: Having gone for refuge to the Buddha, do not pay homage to worldly gods. Having gone for refuge to the Dharma, do not inflict harm or violence on sentient beings. Having gone for refuge to the Sangha, do not rely upon non-Buddhists. These are the three distinguishing precepts.

Then there are the three supporting precepts, which are training in respecting representations in order to gain true dignity: Having gone to the Buddha for refuge, avoid being disrespectful toward drawn or sculpted images of the Buddha, and pay them respect instead. Having gone for refuge to the Dharma, avoid being disrespectful toward a four-line stanza or more of Dharma, and pay them respect instead. Having gone for refuge to the Sangha, avoid being disrespectful toward those in saffron robes who have gone forth, and pay them respect instead. These are the three supporting precepts.

There are five common precepts: In terms of the difficulty of encountering them, train in never rejecting the Three Jewels even at the cost of your life, position, or great effort; and whatever illness, happiness, sorrow, or great need may arise, train in not doing divinations, practicing shamanism, or looking for another method. In terms of fulfilling your needs and wishes, train in offering the first, choicest portion of whatever you eat or drink to the Three Jewels; train in regular worship; train in not taking refuge in or prostrating to the gods of whichever direction you are going. In terms of remembering the benefits, train in taking refuge three times by day and three times by night in order to develop and strengthen it.

Although the benefits of training in these precepts are said to be innumerable, the great Atisha summarized them as eight: becoming Buddhist; being unaffected by harm caused by humans or nonhumans; exhausting and burning up all your misdeeds; gathering a vast accumulation of merit; not falling into the lower realms or bad rebirths upon your death; the superior path being born within you; becoming a support for all the vows; and ultimately achieving unexcelled enlightenment. In sum:

> Becoming Buddhist, the support for vows,
> Human and other harms have no effect,
> Extinguishing misdeeds, increasing merit,
> Not falling to lower realms, distinctive path,
> And achieving unexcelled enlightenment.

The detriments of not going for refuge are the opposite of those. According to Atisha, the meaning of the term is:

Because it is *refuge* from samsara's terrors
And *going* to a place that's unexcelled,
We say the words, "To go for refuge."

That completes the common refuge. Next is aspirational bodhichitta, the resolve of supreme enlightenment. First arrange a mandala and offerings. Seat the lama to whom you make the resolve on a high throne. Prostrate, touching his feet, and recite the supplication:

"Master, please consider me. Just as the tathagata, arhat, completely perfect bhagavan buddhas of the past and the great bodhisattvas who dwell on the high levels first made the resolve to reach unexcelled, completely perfect enlightenment, in the same way, master, please help me develop the resolve to reach unexcelled, completely perfect enlightenment." Make this request three times.

There are four causes for developing aspirational bodhichitta: gathering the accumulation of merit; having previously gone for distinctive refuge; being motivated by distinctive compassion; and conceiving of your lama as a buddha.

To gather the accumulation of merit, visualize that before you in the sky are all the lamas, buddhas, and bodhisattvas sitting on jeweled thrones and lotus and moon seats, and then offer your body and all your possessions to them.

The distinctive refuge is superior to the common refuge due to four distinctions: the duration, the intention, the sources of refuge, and the purpose. Previously in the common refuge, the duration was to go for refuge for the rest of your life. The intention was only for your own sake. The sources of refuge were the form body of the Buddha, the defiled Dharma,[10] and the Sangha of listeners. The purpose was to give rise to the vows of individual liberation. For the distinctive refuge, the distinctive duration is until you reach the essence of enlightenment. The distinctive intention is for the sake of infinite sentient beings. As for the distinctive sources of refuge, the Buddha is the dharmakaya, the Dharma is the nondual nature, and the Sangha is the Sangha of bodhisattvas. The purpose is to give rise to the bodhisattva vow. In this context, conceive of the lama as a buddha and think that you will bring yourself and all infinite sentient beings to achieve unexcelled enlightenment. Think that for that purpose, you will take the Buddha as the teacher, the mahayana Dharma as the path, and bodhisattvas who dwell on the high levels as companions on the path.

Repeat after the master: "All buddhas and bodhisattvas who dwell in the ten directions, please consider me. Master, please consider me. From now until I reach the essence of enlightenment, I, named (*name*), go for refuge to the supreme among those with two feet, the bhagavan buddhas. I go for refuge to peace, the supreme among freedoms from desire, Dharma that is nonabiding nirvana. I go for refuge to the supreme among communities, the noble Sangha of irreversible bodhisattvas." Then the master says, "This is the method," and the students reply, "It is excellent." The precepts are similar to the common precepts.

Next, the limitless compassion of bodhichitta is to think that all the infinite sentient beings have been your mothers. They wander in the ocean of samsara's suffering and deserve compassion, so for the sake of your mothers you will achieve omniscient buddhahood.

Then conceive of your lama as a buddha and repeat after the master: "All buddhas and bodhisattvas who dwell in the ten directions, please consider me. Master, please consider me. Through all the virtue that I, named (*name*), have accomplished since beginningless lifetimes up until now that arises out of generosity, out of discipline, and out of meditation, just as the tathagata, arhat, completely perfect buddhas of the past and the bodhisattvas who dwell on the high levels first made the resolve to reach unexcelled, completely perfect enlightenment, so too shall I, named (*name*), also make the resolve to reach unexcelled, completely perfect enlightenment. I shall liberate sentient beings who have not been liberated, inspire those who have not been inspired, and make those who have not passed into nirvana pass into nirvana." Recite this three times. Then the master says, "This is the method," and the students reply, "It is excellent."

It is not enough merely to rouse bodhichitta; merely performing a ritual is not sufficient. You must train in the precepts. You must train in giving up the four black acts, in employing the four white acts, in not giving up on sentient beings, and in strengthening and cultivating bodhichitta.

The four black acts are: deceiving lamas and those worthy of respect with the intention to mislead; acting with deceit and pretense toward sentient beings; speaking inappropriate words out of hatred to bodhisattvas who have roused bodhichitta; and making others regret things that should not be regretted.

The four white acts are the opposite: not telling lies to lamas and those worthy of respect even at the cost of your life; not acting out of deceit and pretense toward sentient beings with an impure intent; maintaining the conception of bodhisattvas who have developed bodhichitta as teachers and spreading their renown throughout the ten directions; and when you bring sentient beings to virtue, bringing them to unexcelled, completely perfect enlightenment instead of the enlightenment of listeners or self-buddhas.

Not giving up on sentient beings means taking care of others without getting discouraged, even if they harm your body or possessions.

Strengthening and purifying bodhichitta means performing the longer ritual at least three times every day and three times every night. Alternatively, you may perform a shorter ritual.

The benefits:

> If the merit of bodhichitta
> Were to have a form,
> It would fill the whole of space
> And expand even further.

This completes the ritual of going for refuge and rousing bodhichitta, which was recorded from the lama's words.

Dedications for the Living and the Deceased

NAMO RATNA GURU. *In the words of the precious guru:*

It is said that dedicating the roots of goodness is extremely important. If you perform virtue but do not dedicate it, it will become depleted. If you dedicate it to a lesser purpose, it will become depleted. If you regret it, it will become depleted. If you publicize it, it will become depleted. Dedication is the method to prevent virtue from being depleted and to increase and strengthen it.

Regarding the recipient of the dedication, dedications are effective when made in the presence of representations of the Three Jewels. Dedications are effective when made in the presence of someone with bodhichitta. Dedications are effective when made in the presence of your lama.

What you dedicate is all virtue of the three times. This includes all the virtue of the past, present, and future. All the roots of goodness can be summarized as three types: the virtue born of generosity, born of discipline, and born of meditation.

The manner of dedication is not to dedicate virtue for your own self, for this life, or for achieving arhatship or self-buddhahood. Instead dedicate it so that you and all infinite sentient beings achieve unexcelled, completely perfect enlightenment—this is a vast dedication. Its result will never get depleted until you achieve buddhahood. For example, if you spit on a dry rock, the drop of spittle will dry up quickly, but if you spit into the ocean, it will not dry up until the ocean dries up. Similarly, if you dedicate all the virtue you have accumulated in the three times in the presence of your lama and so forth with the intention that you and all infinite sentient beings achieve omniscient buddhahood, the dedication will be accomplished as you have made it. A meaningless thing takes on the highest and best meaning so that it will accomplish a great purpose—it is like a hidden treasure. Therefore, think that all the buddhas and bodhisattvas are present in the sky in front of you. Think to yourself, "I shall make it so that I and all sentient beings achieve omniscient buddhahood. For that purpose, I dedicate all the virtue accumulated in the three times to unexcelled enlightenment."

Repeat after the person leading the dedications: "All buddhas and bodhisattvas dwelling in the ten directions, think of me. Venerable members of the Sangha, I ask that you consider me. Through all the virtue that I, named (*name*), have done, encouraged, or rejoiced in throughout beginningless births up to now, arising from generosity, arising from discipline, and arising from meditation; especially those arising this year from such actions as presenting offerings to the Three Jewels, serving the Sangha, reciting the sutras of the transcendences, offering tormas to Dharma protectors, giving tormas to *bhutas*, and serving feasts to people in my immediate or general area; through these roots of goodness, and through sublime generosity—the ornaments of the mind, the mind's necessities, the collection of yogas, and the supreme purpose[11]—may I attain omniscient buddhahood for the benefit of all innumerable beings, with my preceptor, master, and parents first and foremost." Recite that three times. After the last repetition:

"Until that is attained, in every life, may I acquire a human body with excellent leisure and resources. Having acquired a human body, may I encounter a spiritual friend of the mahayana. After I have received both teaching and instruction from the spiritual friend, may no outer or inner obstacles to their practice arise. May I achieve the supreme siddhi of mahamudra. May it be just so." Recite that three times.

If you wish to make a dedication for the deceased, think that you are dedicating all the virtue they have done in the three times and all the virtue their surviving relatives have done on their behalf so that they, foremost among all sentient beings, are freed from all the suffering of samsara and achieve unexcelled enlightenment. While thinking that, repeat after the person leading the dedications:

"All buddhas and bodhisattvas who abide in the ten directions, I pray that you consider the deceased, (*name*), and all others. Noble members of the Sangha, I pray that you consider the deceased, (*name*). Through all the roots of goodness accumulated throughout the three times by the deceased, (*name*), including those arising from generosity, those arising from discipline, and those arising from meditation; the roots of goodness done, encouraged, and rejoiced in by them; and the roots of goodness done by us, their surviving relatives, for the benefit of the deceased, (*name*), including presenting offerings to the Three Jewels, serving the Sangha, reciting the sutras of transcendent wisdom, offering tormas to Dharma protectors, giving tormas to bhutas, and serving feasts to the people of our immediate or general area; through these roots of goodness, wherever and if the deceased has been born, through the power of karma, among the six types of beings, may these roots of goodness accompany and follow them. May they be freed from all the sufferings of the six types of beings and acquire a human body with excellent leisure and resources. Having acquired a human body, may they hear the sound of the Three Jewels. Having heard the words 'the Three Jewels,' may they acquire faith in the Three Jewels. Having acquired faith in the Three Jewels, may they take refuge, generate bodhichitta, train in all the precepts, and attain omniscient buddhahood." Recite that three times. Those members of the Sangha present should respond three times with, "May it be just so."

Thus dedicating to their benefit those virtues done on their behalf becomes a great virtue for oneself. Therefore, it is said that you should also dedicate the virtue of the living.

This completes the ritual for dedications for the living and deceased, which was recorded from Rinpoche's speech.

A Ritual for the Fasting Vows

NAMO to the gurus.

It is said that no one else has these instructions for giving the fasting vows that descend from the spiritual friend Mahayogi. Once Mahayogi said to Jowo Atisha that people took the fasting vows from Atisha when he was present, but no one had the instructions on how to give fasting vows to faithful male and female sponsors who wished to take them when Atisha was not present. Mahayogi asked Atisha for the instructions, and Atisha was greatly pleased. He said, "Mahayogi Bodhi, I can do that," and then taught the tradition for giving fasting vows. Mahayogi said, "Isn't that the Mahasanghika tradition? Can we Tibetans do that?" Then Atisha's smile turned dark. "That won't help," he said. "You are just making such things up. That is from a quotation in the ritual for giving the vows of going forth in the vinaya. How can the Mahasanghika tradition help you in the Sarvastivada?[12] This was taught by Guru Serlingpa."

It is said that there are the traditions of explanation and of practice for the fasting vows. According to the scriptures:

The individual liberation
Is canceled by returning vows,
Or dying, or two organs arising,
Severing the roots, or passing the night.

This explains that when the night passes, the fasting vows are canceled. However, this is according to the tradition of explanation, it is said. According to the tradition of practice, it is stated that they may be taken for one's whole life, and thus that is allowed.

First, according to the spiritual instructions, the three realms of samsara are suffering by nature. There is not even an instant without suffering. Eliminating all faults and perfecting all qualities is perfect buddhahood. Yet this does not occur without a cause. It does not come from a mistaken cause. It does not occur when the causes are incomplete. It does not occur when blocked by adverse circumstances. The only cause for achieving buddhahood is the three precious trainings. The superior training in discipline is like a completely pure vessel. The superior training in samadhi is like the water contained within it. The superior training in wisdom is like the reflections of the sun and moon appearing in that.

Among the three trainings, the primary one is the superior training in discipline. For lay people, only these fasting vows are important. The Buddha said to the great king Prasenajit, "Great King, you have so many things to do that you are unable to train in the six transcendences. Therefore, train in keeping the eight branches of the fasting vows."

The noble Nagarjuna as well said to the great king Surabhibhadra:

> Practice discipline without lapse,
> Without transgression, mixing, or taint.
> Like the earth for beings who move or who do not,
> Discipline is the basis for all qualities.

Thus he told the king to abide by the eight branches of the fasting vows.

The master should say, "Since the fasting vows are important, repeat after me."

Recite three times: "Master, please consider me. From this time onward as long as I live, I, named (*name*), go for refuge to the supreme among those with two feet, the Buddha. I go for refuge to the supreme among freedoms from desire, the Dharma. I go for refuge to the supreme among all communities, the Sangha."

Recite three times: "Master, please consider me. From this time onward as long as I live, please accept me, named (*name*), as one who fasts on the full moon, new moon, or eighth day of every month."

The master says: "This is the method." The disciples respond, "It is excellent." That bestows the vow.

Then say: "It is not enough just to take the vows; you must keep them. If you do not keep them, it is like picking up a stone from the ground and striking your own head. Thus, so that you know what must be kept, repeat the precepts.

"Master, please consider me. Just as the noble arhats of the past gave up taking life; taking what is not given; unchaste acts; telling lies; beer brewed from grain, fermented drinks, and intoxicants that bring carelessness; song, dance, music, necklaces, and wearing perfumes and colored ornaments; high beds and great seats; and eating after noon, thus turning away from eating after noon, so, too, do I, named (*name*), from this time onward as long as I live, on the full moon, new moon, or eighth day of every month, give up taking life; taking what is not given; unchaste acts; telling lies; beer brewed from grain, fermented drinks, and intoxicants that bring carelessness; song, dance, music, necklaces, and wearing perfumes and colored ornaments; high beds and great seats; and eating after noon. I turn away from eating after noon. Through these eight branches, I shall train in the precepts of the noble arhats. I shall accomplish them. I shall do them."

The master says: "This is the method." The disciples respond, "It is excellent."

These are what need to be kept, so wash early in the morning. Then think that there are innumerable buddhas and bodhisattvas present in the sky in front of you and prostrate as many times as you can.

On that day, do not harm any living creature. If you kill a human being on that day, your vows are completely broken. However, it is not appropriate to kill anything even as small as an ant. With taking what is not given, if you steal something worth more than one dre of grain from another, the vow is broken. However, it is not appropriate to steal anything even as small as the husk of a sesame seed. If you perform any action that is not chaste, your vows are completely broken. However, even looking lustfully at a woman is not appropriate. If you tell a lie such as that you saw gods whom you had not seen, achieved arhatship when you had not, or so forth, you have broken the vows completely. However, do not tell lies even as a joke or to tease someone. The vows are the antidote to these actions. These are the four root precepts, and they are similar to a tree: if you cut a tree at its roots, the branches will also wither.

You do not completely break your vows if you drink beer brewed from grain and so forth, but that causes the vows to lapse and therefore become ineffective, so you must keep this precept well. If you do not, it is said that in your next life you will have to drink boiling molten metal.

In Tibet, song, dance, playing music, necklaces, perfume, wearing ornaments, high beds, and great seats do not exist as generally known in the world, but it is said that the intent to give them up brings merit.

Giving up food after noon means that after the sun has reached its zenith until the next dawn, it is not appropriate for those who are not sick to eat even suitable food.

The practices of enhancing the essence and eliminating negative influences are Tibetan inventions. Therefore you should only go for refuge.

This completes the ritual for going for fasting vows, which was recorded from the lama's speech.

Dusum Khyenpa's Life Story in One Hundred and Eight Vignettes

With the two accumulations complete, you know three
kayas to be spontaneously present.
Appearance and emptiness inseparable, you abide in the
dharmakaya.
Great bliss free of elaboration, this radiant clarity
continues without break.
You see all to be known in the three times with
vajra eyes.

You are Vajradhara, the essential nature of all the
buddhas,
Lord of Dharma, for whom emptiness and compassion
never part.
Through numerous emanations, you fully benefit others.
I bow in respect to the unequaled Precious One.

Here begins the precious lama's spiritual biography, *Dusum Khyenpa's Life Story in One Hundred and Eight Vignettes.*

1

"I remember being born in the realm of Beryl Blue in the eastern part of this world realm and being a fully ordained monk."

2

"I was born in Dharitha, an island between the southern continent of the Rose Apple and the western continent of the Bountiful Cow. At that time, Gampopa Rinpoche was the yogi Surapa, and in his presence, I gave rise to the resolve of bodhichitta."

3

"After this, I was born in Uddiyana, found in the west of India and belonging to this Rose Apple Continent. I was known as the yogi Utita, a natural yogi. I had no master and gave no oral instructions, yet I was very powerful."

4

"Then I was born into the Brahmin caste on the western continent of the Bountiful Cow. When I became fully ordained, I received the name Dharma Atita, and my secret name was Dharmashri. I benefited some living beings, and my lama at that time was Telopa."

5

"After that, I took birth as an elephant on the western continent of the Bountiful Cow. The king Dharmashila, who was not a Buddhist, was undermining the Buddhist teachings. So once when some seven hundred elephants went out to make war, this elephant was at the head of the troops and trampled the non-Buddhist king to death. The intention here was to benefit the Buddha's teachings and to rescue from the lower realms this king who was acting like a despot. In a later life, he became my disciple and now is the patron Gönpawa."

6

"I was born next in the Indian kingdom of Kalingka as the king Dawa Nampar Nönpa. At that time, Gampopa was named Sangye Yeshe Shap, and his master was Jampal Shenyen Avadhutipa.

"Once, when I was going to circumambulate the Glorious Drepung Stupa, these words resonated from the sky: 'You have not yet attained the siddhis. Go elsewhere and gather the conditioned roots of goodness.' And so I established a monastery for many monks and gathered great virtue and its causes. Then I returned and circumambulated the stupa many times." It is said that thereby he attained all siddhis without exception.

"At that time, the emanation of Jampal Shenyen Avadhutipa was Lama Milarepa. Sangye Yeshe Shap was Gampopa. In *The History of the Pak Kor Guhyasamaja* this is told differently."

7

"After this, I took birth on the Rose Apple Continent near a river known as Adorned with Lotus Flowers, located at the farthest reaches of the northwest. I was known as Bhikshu Dharmakirti and my spiritual teacher was the Brahmin Sajjana. I also served as an abbot for others, including Geshe Takdeuwa. A few of them are here in this group as well. At that time, I supplicated the master Dombipa, who was residing on Bird Shelter Rocky Mountain, and my wishes were fulfilled."

8

"Subsequently, I was born on the eastern continent of Superior Body as Sherap Sangmo, the daughter of the king Gewa Sangpo. My secret name was Tsokye Bodhi." (It is said that the reason he was born as a daughter is that if he had been born as a son, he would have been obligated to take over the kingdom.) "During that time, Gampopa was Bhikshu Dharmasiddhi. Having received vows from him, I kept them properly. I gave all the many possessions I had to Gampopa, which pleased him, and he gave whatever Dharma teaching I requested."

9

"After this birth, I was born in a city called Rajaphala (also known as the City of the Excellent King) on the island Radhapala, which was not famous like the subcontinents. It was located between the eastern continent of Superior Body and the southern continent of the Rose Apple at its southeastern border. My father was Dharmagupta and my mother Sumati, and I was called Pratikirti. We belonged to the merchant caste. At full ordination, I received the name Bhikshu Ratnashila and lived for one hundred sixty-four years." It is said that he was a practitioner of great power.

"During this life, my lama was Palgyi Bepa, who was an incarnation of Gampopa. Among my students were many Kadampas. I taught *Clearly Distinguishing Dharma Empowerments*, a text that was as beneficial then as it is now."

10

Afterward, at the very center of the billion worlds, in the middle of the southern Rose Apple Continent, is the Vajra Seat. Located to its north in the land of the kingdom of snow is Treshö, a lotuslike country encircled by snowy mountains; within it is an area known as Pochu Dong Karpo—the birthplace of Dusum Khyenpa. His father was called Gompa Dorje Gönpo, his mother Lhatokpa, and he was given the name Gepel.

11

From Gompa Gepo and his father, Dusum Khyenpa received the practice "Accomplishing the Life Force of Palden Lhamo's Heart. "

12

Meeting Lama Berotsana and Paldzin, he received many key instructions and also teachings on the Protector,[13] written by the Brahmin Vararuchi.

13

Through his practice of Palden Lhamo, all the signs of accomplishment arose and he had a clear vision of her.

14

In the village of Duru, he had an enemy. This person had gone up to Domdom Ridge to take care of some business and on the way down, he was dragged along the ground by a horse and killed. As an offering of thanks to the Dharma protectors, Dusum Khyenpa galloped away on a horse, holding a fluttering flag.

15

When he was sixteen, he took monastic vows from the great abbot Chokgi Lama and the master Chak Senge Drak at Chökhor Chenpo Kadrak. He was given the name Shramanera Dharmakirti (Chökyi Drakpa). For a short while, he participated in the Sangha's activities and set up a small place where he practiced.

16

From Yolchö Wang, a disciple of Jowo Atisha, and his disciple and vajra brother Geshe Trarawa, Dusum Khyenpa received the Chakrasamvara empowerment in Atisha's tradition and numerous sadhanas of the secret mantrayana.

17

At the age of nineteen, begging for alms along the way, he went to Central Tibet to study and contemplate. At Yorpö Nyamo Gyur lived Geshe Tölung Gyamar. From him and his disciple Geshe Chappa, Dusum Khyenpa listened to teachings on the three Madhyamikas from the east (Shantarakshita's *Ornament of the Middle Way*, Yeshe Nyingpo's *Two Truths in the Middle Way*, and Kamalashila's *Illumination of the Middle Way*), and he also studied the *Five Dharmas of Maitreya*.

18

In Penyul, he met Geshe Sharawa and his disciple, the

yogi Sherap Dorje. For six years, he studied and contemplated numerous Kadampa teachings.

19

In the cave of Tongsa, he took full ordination. The abbot was the great Vinaya Holder Mel, the master was Yeshe Lodrö, and the private questioner was the abbot's younger brother. Dusum Khyenpa studied the vinaya and then taught it to others.

20

He said that in Gyal Lhakhang, he received teachings from Lama Pal Galo and Khampa Aseng on the six applications and the black protector Female Crow as well as others.

21

Traveling to Dakpo, he met Geshe Shawa Lingpa and Pandita Gompa, who were in residence at the monastery of Drakha. He heard them teach *The Four Seats*.

22

At the age of thirty-three, Dusum Khyenpa journeyed to Daklha Monastery but was not allowed to meet Gampopa for nearly two months. When he finally did, he offered ten white scarves and requested key instructions. Gampopa gave him a short teaching on path and fruition, saying, "I meditated on this, and you should, too." Master Gomtsul served as Dusum Khyenpa's assistant, providing him with all his basic needs.

After he received key instructions on the path of method, Dusum Khyenpa meditated for nine days and warmth arose.

For the next nine months, he wore only cotton cloth. Then Gampopa said, "Go to Sangri to meditate." He meditated there for three months during the summer and said that his mind rested stably however he might direct it and that his practice of insight was like the sun and moon appearing from behind the clouds.

Having paid respects to his lama, Dusum Khyenpa meditated for three years at the monastery itself while also undergoing great hardship. He became known as one of the toughest among the eight hundred meditators. Many marvelous signs of the path arose for him. Delighted, he went to pay respects to his teacher and engage in dialogue about his meditative experience. He came into the presence of Gampopa at Jagö Retreat and gave his report. Gampopa responded, "Alas! Khampa Gray Hair, I had great hopes in you, but you're quite mistaken. Go back and meditate more." Dusum Khyenpa thought, "There's no mistake here," and six more months of meditation produced nothing new. Then he went back to his lama: "Even if I meditated for one hundred years, it would not generate anything new in mind's essential nature. Even if I'm mistaken, I'm going to meditate like this." Gampopa was delighted: "You have cut the ties to samsara." He then introduced Dusum Khyenpa to the depth of mind's abiding nature and gave him further key instructions to support his practice.

23

When Dusum Khyenpa went to Loro, he met Lama Rechungpa and received teachings on establishing sessions and the six dharmas. He shone brilliantly in a dialogue about

Naropa's key instructions. He also received key instructions from another of Lord Milarepa's disciples, Tsemo Namkha Salja.

24

From a disciple of Jowo Atisha, Rompa Gargey, and from his disciple, Yönpukpa Töngyal, Dusum Khyenpa received Vajra Varahi along with the related Dharma practices, *Rinchen Gyendrup, Wangshi Nyamgom*, and other texts. From Gyapmo Pangkhawa, a disciple of Metsönpo, he heard instructions and explanations about Hevajra.

25

Further, at Luk Pukmoche, he received teachings from Geshe Dorseng on path and fruition. From Geshe Ralchak Töntsul of Daryul he heard many instructions on glorious Chakrasamvara and Sangkar Lotsawa's teachings.

26

Then Gampopa told Dusum Khyenpa, "Go to Ölkhar Retreat." He went to a cave on Ölkhar Dreu Riwoche, and as soon as he arrived there, a woman appeared and said, "Don't stay here. My mistress is coming." Thinking that she was an ogress living in the cave, Rinpoche meditated on love and compassion. After he practiced in this place for four months, a special certainty arose in his mind and he sang the song of realization called "Mind at Ease."

27

When receiving a profound empowerment from the Lord of Dharma Gampopa, he had a vision of the resplendent kaya of Hevajra, which was circled in light. Further, all four of his Dharma companions who received the empowerment from Gomtsul saw him as the Glorious Heruka, appearing the same to all of them. When they told this to Gomtsul, he said, "The Heruka is me." He had six pure visions of Master Gomtsul, three times as Hevajra, as Vajra Yogini, and as a mass of light.[14]

28

Gampopa advised Dusum Khyenpa, "Go meditate in Mön." So he carried five dre of salt and traveled to see Katung, the king of Mön. One of the queen's female servants was a distant relative of Dusum Khyenpa's and served as his translator when he met the king in person and offered the salt. The king extended his support to Rinpoche, and so he went to live in the mountains of Mön.

One time when he had run out of food, he was walking down a path that led out of the mountains and a tiger emerged from the woods. Rinpoche was sitting on the uppermost part of a large boulder as the tiger circumambulated him and left. Seeing that it would not harm him, Dusum Khyenpa continued down the path and met two young women, who offered him a half gourd filled with nectar. Arriving at the king's palace, he replenished his supplies and returned to the mountains. At this time he composed a song about the border between Mön and Tibet.[15] When Dusum Khyenpa left for Tibet, as parting gifts the king offered him several bolts of valuable cloth and a mantra against poison.
Arriving at Dakpo, Dusum Khyenpa meet Gampopa, who asked, "Did a tiger circumambulate you?"

"Yes, it did."

"The tiger was an emanation of a dakini. The two young women who offered you nectar were dakinis associated with the local protectors. They gave you siddhis." Dusum Khyenpa spent a year at Gampo.

29

He asked his lama, "I'd like to look around the country," and Gampopa replied, "Go ahead." While touring, Rinpoche opened a new path to Nyal, and then, passing through Lhodrak, he arrived at Palri. He befriended four Khampas, with whom he traveled back to Pakri in Gö. At a few passes, they prepared food and drink. Two of them went to gather wood while the other two set up the hearth. At that time, lightning cracked through the sky and struck the two out in front, killing both of them. To accumulate merit for the two deceased, the remaining two Khampas offered two lengths of woolen cloth to Dusum Khyenpa, who experienced all this as if it were a dream.

30

Then he went to the area of Dhar Minyak in Western Tibet. Living there in an earthen cave were two brothers, both novice monks and disciples of Milarepa. From them Rinpoche received key instructions, and the younger brother offered him instruction on mahamudra from the tradition of his master, Lord Milarepa.

31

Subsequently Dusum Khyenpa journeyed to Penyul and practiced for three summers and winters sealed into a cave at

Jasang Rock. Immeasurable qualities of the yoga of inner heat arose, and he became known as the "Lama of the Rock." In the way he appeared to others, he seemed to pass without obstruction through mountains and boulders. He had visions of many yidam deities.

32

Gampopa advised him, "You should go to meditate at Jomo Gangkar." Below Pabong Karlep, a retreat of Master Padmasambhava, he passed the summer engaged in the practice of extracting the essence, and many qualities arose in his mindstream. When the thought of his lama as the Buddha arose, he sang a song in six vajra verses.[16] During that period, he continually saw the local deity Dzomo Karyuma.

Dusum Khyenpa said, "If you lack devotion, positive qualities will not arise in your mindstream. I have never thought of my lama as ordinary."

33

That fall in Nyemo Nyidrung, he came down a ravine to a place near a fort. Close to a house appeared four young women who were weaving. One of them said, "Master, will you have something to eat?"

"Yes," he replied.

One of them went inside and said, "Come in!"

"Bring it out here," he requested.

"Nothing bad will happen. Do come in," she said. When he went inside, all four young women were there. They offered him food and drink in a half gourd resembling a skull cup. On the thumbs of the young woman who prepared the meal, he saw Chakrasamvara with four faces and twelve hands, embraced by his consort.

The meal was a stew of human fingers. Without hesitation, he consumed everything and found it extremely delicious. Then one of the young women raised to the sky a cup filled with a milky liquid. She offered it to him and he drank it. It was like ambrosia. Then, just as he arrived at the door of the house, the four young women appeared outside, weaving again, near the gate of the fence that encircled the house. Walking down the road from there, Dusum Khyenpa experienced the earth soft as a silk cushion, his body light as cotton, and his mind knew a happiness free of identifying things as this or that.

34

Between Shu and Nye, in a hermitage known as Dzong, he met a woman meditator who was tending cattle.

"Who lives in that retreat up there?" he asked her.

"My master stays there," she replied.

"I'd like to meet him."

"He's in retreat."

"I absolutely have to meet him."

"I'll go ask," she said and left. Returning, she said, "Please go up."

When he went inside, he found an older man and woman who were ordained. As he was prostrating, the lama made a sign that he should not, indicating the nun, but Dusum Khyenpa made prostrations anyway.

When they had sat down, the Lama Dzongpa said, "Did four young women offer you a meal today?"

"They did."

"They all were dakinis. The contents of the stew were taken by the dakinis in Pamting, Nepal. They're from the corpse of the householder Ashoka's son Dharmasiddhi, which was being carried to the charnel ground of Tartita."

"Are they here now?"

"No, they're not. They went to the charnel ground of the Kashmiri city Sambhata. It is a place where the dakinis gather on the twenty-fifth of the black month, so they traveled there for ceremonies. These dakinis bestowed siddhis on you. On the road in Mön, the two young women who offered you drink were also dakinis."

Rinpoche thought, "His solitary retreat here resembles my lama's Par Tsang retreat."

The lama said, "Does this retreat resemble your lama's Par Tsang retreat?" With this, Rinpoche did not dare to have other thoughts. They conversed about many things.

Lama Dzongpa asked, "You should do whatever your lama Gampopa says." He also made a prophecy. Dusum Khyenpa received from him "The Lightning-Strike Mahamudra" and many key instructions. Lama Dzongpa belonged to the third generation of Naropa's disciples.

35

When staying in Drushi Retreat, Dusum Khyenpa heard that the Lord of Dharma Gampopa's physical form had dissolved, so he departed for Daklha. At the monastery in Ölkha named Porok Dzongchung, he met Lama Gomtsul and Master Pakpa. He clutched Lama Gomtsul's robes and shed tears. To pacify his torment, Gampopa himself, who had just passed away, appeared within a rainbow in the sky. Seeing this, the master and two disciples prostrated, and at that moment it faded away.

36

At Drushi Retreat he engaged many times in the fasting practice, "The Meaningful Lasso."[17] Through repeatedly practicing the approach and accomplishment phases related to Vajra Varahi, he had a vision of her with two faces and surrounded by her retinue.

37

One night at Drushi Retreat, he 'dreamt that a huge serpent was pursuing him. Though he tried to escape, it followed him all the way down to the ocean's depths and all the way up to the peak of Mount Meru. As Rinpoche was about to fly into the sky, the serpent swallowed him up. Glancing back over his shoulder, Rinpoche saw that his big toes remained outside the serpent's mouth.

Then his attendant Jowo Yeshe Ö came close to Rinpoche. He had noticed that the elder great meditator was sleeping but his sleep was unusual as if he were subdued by a demon.

He asked, "What's happening?"

"I had an unusual dream," Rinpoche replied and related it.

"You looked like an ordinary person oppressed by a demon."

A few days later, Dusum Khyenpa said to this attendant,

"That dream was a good one. Previously, I had to maintain my samadhi with mindfulness. After that dream, I no longer need to do that. But for a few days, I had to maintain the samadhi because I had looked at the toes left outside. This dream was a sign that through the interdependence of the channels, winds, and mind, the winds and mind had entered into the central channel." It is said that he then acted like a little child.

38

At Tsurgi Ngösang, his tooth was aching. From it came many smaller teeth that some time later turned into numerous relics shaped as stupas, vajras, and mustard seeds. In particular, the forms of the Glorious Heruka, Vajra Yogini, and Khasarpani came forth. Depending on outer circumstances, it also happened that they multiplied or disappeared.

39

"Lord Gampopa had said to me, 'You should go one time to Kampo Gangra.' I started to go, but the moment I arrived at Mikmang in Ölkha, my leg gave me trouble. The Dharma protectors were not allowing me to go. Later, Lama Gomtsul also said, 'Since these were the lama's words, you should go to Kampo Gangra whether it's delightful or miserable.'"

Gya Akyap, a traveler from Trewo, invited Dusum Khyenpa to his monastery. As they traveled down the northern route, one night in a dream, Rinpoche found the plump corpse of a woman and cut it open. From the base of her ribs came naturally arising sounds of damarus, lifting into space. Rinpoche departed together with these and arrived in the country of Uddiyana. A young woman said to him, "From here onward is the region of the wisdom dakinis, and from here downward is the region of the worldly dakinis." He heard many key instructions to support his practice.

40

He had a vision at Kampo Nenang of Hevajra and eight deities. He also heard teachings on *The Praise to Hevajra in Eight Verses* and advice on the bardo.

41

At Kampo Nenang he had a clear vision of Coemergent Hevajra.

42

In Pompuk to the south of Palgyi Ri, he had a vision of a naked Vajra Yogini experiencing bliss, with her hair flowing free. Without ornaments, she held a skull cup and curved knife while her right leg rested in the crook of her left elbow. She was the unadorned Khechari.

43

At Kampo Nenang, he had a clear vision of Tara the Wish-Fulfilling Wheel.

44

At another time, Rinpoche went to the Grove of the Roaming Buffalo to the north of Bodhgaya. He met Master Gomtsul, who said, "It's amazing that you have the ability to come here." They discussed many things and Rinpoche also heard many key instructions.

45

At Kampo Nenang he had a vision of Vajra Yogini with one thousand heads and one thousand hands, encircled by thirty-six heroines. She said:

> In the tantra of the Heruka,
> The mind is said to be free of stains.
> A pure emanation of Dharma
> Has arisen in the form of Varahi.

46

At Kampo Nenang, the first fall (or seventh) month, Dusum Khyenpa was commemorating his lama Gampopa. When half a day had passed, numerous rainbow parasols and mandalas appeared. Right in front of them, Lama Rinpoche and the attendants Lekdze and Drakdze were present as part of the principal deity's retinue. Gampopa said:

> Son, the main point of the view is nonduality.
> The main point of meditation is nondistraction.
> The main point of conduct is union.
> The main point of the result is the three undivided.

So saying, he vanished.

47

After numerous forms of ĀLI and KĀLI had appeared in the sky at Nenang, he saw Nairatmya and the fourteen goddesses.

48

While residing at Kampo Nenang, he turned his mind to Sri Lanka. There in a charnel ground he met a master with vajra and bell. After supplicating him, Rinpoche received what he had wished for.

49

At Kampo Nenang he saw noble Achala in union with the goddess Nairatmya.

50

While at at Kampo Nenang, he dreamt that a fully ordained monk, who was all white, appeared and said, "I'm going to hear the Dharma from a buddha."

Rinpoche thought, "Dipamkara and Shakyamuni are not present in this world," so he asked, "Is it the victorious Maitreya you're going to see?"

"I am," came the reply. The two flew to Tushita on the rays of the sun. In a sambhoghakaya form with ornaments, Maitreya was teaching the Dharma to white monks who were all fully ordained. Rinpoche heard:

> In this, there's nothing to remove
> Nor anything at all to add.
> Looking authentically at the authentic
> And seeing authentically is liberation.

Rinpoche said, "I also received instructions on generating supreme bodhichitta."

51

At Kampo Nenang he had a vision of the fierce Amrita Kundali and eight deities in union with their consorts.

52

In another dream at Kampo Nenang, Rinpoche was experiencing bliss while sitting upon a stack of one hundred rocks. In front of him, eight dakinis clad in bone ornaments were offering flower garlands. When tossed into the sky, they transformed into an abode of layered lotus flowers made of jewels.

53

Dechung Sangye had gone to Lhotö, begging for alms along the way. When he arrived at Kampo Nenang, he reported that he had heard Daklha Gampo, Gampopa's main seat, had been destroyed. Dusum Khyenpa focused his attention and looked. First he saw Dakpo clearly, then Nepal, and finally in many directions—above and below plus all the cardinal and intermediate ones—he saw numerous pure lands of the buddhas. Space was filled with buddhas, the Bhagavan Shakyamuni and others, as well as with bodhisattvas. Rinpoche said, "It's not true that the main seat was destroyed."

54

At Kampo Nenang he 'dreamt of Gampopa, who was staying under a rock overhang on a mountain in India. Rinpoche met him and asked, "Lama, were you miraculously born?"

"I was born from a womb," he said.

"Do you have a master?"

"The natural state is uninterrupted, so there's no need for a master," Gampopa replied. He gave Rinpoche this Dharma teaching:

Giving up your place of birth, you'll surely be free of desire and hatred.
With real discipline, you'll surely go to the higher realms.
Applying yourself to skillful means, you'll surely move along the path.
Resting within the natural ground without altering, you'll surely realize the actual nature.

55

At Kampo Nenang he had a vision of Mahamaya and four deities.

56

One night at Kampo Nenang, Rinpoche 'dreamt that he was sitting in an open lotus on a large lake. From all directions came the sound of lutes, played by the eight goddesses of Hevajra. In these lovely tones came their invitation: "From the western direction comes great bliss." He said that this omen of death was reversed.

57

While Dusum Khyenpa was traveling along the road leading from Kampo Nenang to a place that the patron Kyagön had requested him to consecrate, Rinpoche had a clear vision of billowing clouds of Dharma protectors including Palden Lhamo.

58

During the main part of the consecration, the sounds of damarus and ĀLI and KĀLI resounded throughout the sky.

Looking up, Dusum Khyenpa saw numerous gatherings of deities and heard this Dharma teaching:

> View and meditation are like sky and water.
> Conduct cannot be negated or established.
> The natural state is the three inseparable.
> Like the sounds of lutes on a relative level,
> What they are and reality itself are inseparable.

Others also had experiences that transcended words: flowers offered themselves and remained on the statues; the earth moved, shook, and quaked; and lights, sounds, and so forth arose.

59

At Kampo Nenang the protector Drigukma clearly appeared above a great snow mountain in the midst of many curved knives swirling in a dark black cloud.

60

At Kampo Nenang Rinpoche said, "Once the Great Brahmin Saraha and other masters from an earlier time as well as Milarepa, Gampopa and other lamas from a later time gathered to hold a feast offering. I saw them all."

61

He 'dreamt at Kampo Nenang that he wished to see the Kashmiri city of Dripten, so he created hundreds of thousands of emanations of his physical form. Sitting on a swan and lion throne, he arrived in the sky above the Kashmiri city and heard a wave of sweet, unborn sounds.

62

At Kampo Nenang after offering the evening torma, Dusum Khyenpa was conversing with his attendant Mönlam. All of a sudden a red light descended from the wooden planks in the roof of the house. It seemed that Rinpoche's mind became unclear and muddled. The moment he thought it was a dream, it was purified.

Rinpoche was forgetting people's names and so on, and queried his attendant, "What's the name of the young monk with agile hands? And the name of his abbot?"

"His name is Drakpa Sherap and his abbot's name is Tsöndru Sherap."

Then appearances returned to normal and Rahula was not able to inflict his harm.

63

At Kampo Nenang Rinpoche said, "If this water from the snowmelt gives me a goiter, it would be best to go to Central Tibet." That night he 'dreamt that Genyen Dorje Paltsek appeared as a white man with his palms joined together and mounted on a white horse. He said, "These eight plant and liquid medicines are beneficial." So saying, he showed the medicines to Dusum Khyenpa and said, "Please don't always say you have to go. It makes my mind uneasy." Then he left.

Later, when Dusum Khyenpa said he was leaving anyway, this genyen projected many magical displays: He sent down great winds and lightning which split open boulders at Treo Gyuktang and felled numerous pine trees, blocking the road.

64

When Dusum Khyenpa was seventy-four years old, he moved from Kampo Nenang in order to benefit others. After he had traveled up from Drilung, he stayed with all his traveling companions in the hidden land of Sakter Kun. He brought to fruition Jang Kyawa, the geshe of that place, and others. Rinpoche had a vision of Hayagriva and four deities.

65

He spent that summer at Lhongdra, where all the Sangha of Dridampa Chöchuk assembled, and he established them on the path that matures and liberates. Then he went to Tre and remained there for eighteen months, maturing and liberating the people there. At Gampo, he made an offering of seven large turquoises and forty-two containers of tea. Dusum Khyenpa then journeyed to Drilung and finally stayed at Chebar. He established in maturation and liberation about one thousand ordained monks who had assembled. Afterward Rinpoche went to Damen and stayed at Letu Karmar, where he reconciled disputes. He also released all those in prison and benefited many people. He offered the monastery at Gampo *The Prajnaparamita in One Hundred Thousand Verses* written in gold along with some turquoise and silver. Afterward he benefited beings and, traveling to Central Tibet, he created a new road that passed through the south.

In general, he gave to Gampo one hundred ten volumes written in gold, ten large turquoises, and fifty dzo and horses. Principally to the statues of the Jowo Avalokiteshvara and Lhasa's Shakyamuni and also to the geshes of the main monasteries in Ütsang, he offered more than one hundred head of livestock including seventy horses.

66

One day, while he was staying in Tsur Lhalung, in the first month of the spring of the Bird Year, Rinpoche said, "Last night I 'dreamt that I went to an Indian charnel ground where several Indian yogis had gathered to practice together." At that time, he had a clear vision of Avalokiteshvara.

67

When asked for the names of the country in India, the charnel ground, and the sponsor of the feast offering, Dusum Khyenpa responded, "The country was Jalandhara in southern India, the charnel ground was Hahadrokpa, the sponsor was the king Dawa Nampar Nönpa, and the master of the feast offering was Krishnacharya. Among the accomplished masters, the four from India were Krishnacharya, Indrabodhi, Jalandhara, and Shinglopa. The two from Tibet were Dharmashila and Kirti." He dreamt that he went from Western Tibet to Surik.

68

Around the same time, while the teacher of Tangchung Temple in Western Tibet was sewing robes in the main shrine hall, three wandering Indian mendicants appeared, wearing only cotton cloth and carrying skull cups. They were accompanied by a barefoot Tibetan yogi with conch-shell earrings. About sixty years old, he wore just cotton cloth and carried a skull cup and cane made of wood with metal caps on either end. So there were four yogis in all. The Tibetan yogi and the teacher talked a great deal with each other.

"Where did you come from?" asked the teacher.

The Tibetan yogi replied, "On the way here, I came through Bodhgaya, Kashmir, and Purang."

"Why did you go to India?"

"I went for a great ceremony in Bodhgaya."

"Well, I heard that many realized masters came to the memorial services for the Year of the Bird. Did you meet them?"

"At that time," replied the Tibetan, "in the city of Jalandhara in southern India, the king Dawa Nampar Nönpa was celebrating a feast offering at the charnel ground of Hahadrokpa. Supplications were made to yogis who were realized masters and who possessed both the clairvoyances and the ability to perform miracles. Four of them came from India. The lama Mitra Jogi has said that there were also two from Tibet for a total of six."

"Who were they?" the teacher asked.

"The four from India were Indrabodhi, Jalandhara, Krishnacharya, and Shingpopa. There were two from Tibet, Dharmashila and Dharmakirti."

"Who are they?"

"Dharmashila, or Chökyi Tsultrim, has the instructions on achieving immortality and is benefiting others in western Ngari through building a temple. Shri Dharmakirti, or Chökyi Drakpa, has the key instructions on the sufficient and decisive path of mahamudra based on the paths of the channels and winds. He resides in the lower part of Tibet. It seems that he is famous as Lama Gray Hair. We are going there."

"Lama Gray Hair is very famous," the teacher responded. "I was also thinking of going to see him, but I heard that he would not stay long in this world and would soon depart for another place. I doubted I could hear a complete Dharma teaching, so I couldn't make up my mind. I made no plans to go but was not comfortable staying either."

The yogi asked, "Haven't you seen this sutra?" He recited:

For the sake of one disciple
The Buddha remains for an aeon
And also swiftly brings that person to maturity
Just like a seedling given warmth and moisture.

He explained, "If you supplicate for the benefit of others, the buddhas will remain for aeons. Never part from faith and devotion. Go quickly now to the lama. You will receive the entire teaching."

Happy at this, the teacher asked the yogi for key instructions. From nearby one of the mendicants, the yogi picked up a text written on birch paper and explained it to the teacher. Then the yogi gave him the text, saying: "This is a profound key instruction, known as 'The Four Aspects That Can Free the Mindstream and Bring Forth Blessings and Power.' Keep it for yourself and do not show it to others. Later you will meet me again." With these words, he departed.

The teacher returned to his house thinking that in the morning he would invite the yogis to a Dharma feast. He called the caretaker of the temple, who said, "After you left, all the yogis departed as well." Though many looked for the yogis everywhere, no one had seen or heard of them. The teacher was then convinced and made preparations to go see Lama Gray Hair.

In the middle summer month of the Dog Year, the teacher went to Tölung Tsurphu. When he arrived there, Dusum Khyenpa had already recounted to all the monks brief stories of what had happened. The teacher wondered if the four yogis from before had come. But Dusum Khyenpa said, "You can ask that tomorrow morning," so he did not dare to question.

Then thinking, "I should get rid of these doubts," the teacher arranged all the articles for a feast in the house of Drakseng, a chieftain from Kham. The teacher invited Dusum Khyenpa and about ten older monks, including Lama Takdeuwa, Geshe Könchok Senge, and Gompa Tsultrim Gyalpo. During the ceremony, the teacher asked Rinpoche to tell about the four previous yogis, so he gave the stories in detail just as they had happened, and all were amazed.

The teacher asked, "Who were the three wandering mendicants?"

"The middle Indrabodhi, Shinglopa, and Krishnacharya," Rinpoche replied. "I was the one who taught Dharma to you. I had received that oral instruction from Indrabodhi. The vajra master of the Indian feast was Krishnacharya. You have been my disciple in four lifetimes. This is the fifth time we have met. It is excellent that you studied and explained Dharma. But if we hadn't met this time, you would have been lost in a world of explanations. I came to cut through your doubts and get you to meditate."

69

Geshe Takdeu asked, "How is it that this teacher Geshe Tsangpowa met you during four lifetimes?"

Dusum Khyenpa replied, "Previously in India, he was born as the smith Ratnashila, and he generated bodhichitta as my disciple."

70

"Afterward when he was born to the north of this continent, I was his abbot."

71

"Then when he took birth as Metok Sherap Sangpo on the continent of Superior Body, I explained to him the key instruction 'Prajna: the Sessions of Six Dharmas.'"

72

"The life before this one, he was born as the Brahmin Gyalwa Sherap in a remote area of India on the seacoast. I gave him all four empowerments. He was knowledgeable about the treatises and acquired the imprints for meditation, so it was easy for him to develop certainty in view and meditation.

73

Rinpoche related, "Some people say that the king of Minyak is the reincarnation of Geshe Langri Tangpa, but this is not the case. He is the reincarnation of the yogi Matangki. The purpose of his rebirth as a prince was to assist his father the king and to encourage the people of the kingdom to engage in meritorious activity. In addition, by becoming a powerful king, he could release many prisoners who would become his future disciples."

Further, Rinpoche said to Geshe Tsangpowa, "You should depart for the kingdom of Minyak and meditate at Mount Hala Shan. This will bring benefit to many living beings."

74

Rinpoche stated, "There are four reasons I came to Cental Tibet. Master Gomtsul said, 'You should come up from Kham.' I also thought of offering one hundred texts to Gampo. Further, I was thinking of building a monastery here between Shu and Tsur. And then Lama Shang Tsalwa was quarreling with the great meditators and not listening, so I wanted to request him to stop."

Having said this, Rinpoche went to Tsal. While he was reconciling those who were at odds with each other, Lama Shang Tsalwa had many pure visions of Dusum Khyenpa. Joyful, the lama clutched Rinpoche's hand and danced about. Until his death, Lama Shang Tsalwa never quarreled again.

75

One night at Tsurphu Dusum Khyenpa 'dreamt that traveling from Ngari to Surik, he went to an outlying district known as Butana. There he met two yogis, a teacher and his attendant.

"Who are you?" Rinpoche asked.

The teacher replied, "I am Indrabodhi."

Rinpoche supplicated him and received key instructions. He was also taught the sadhana of the Jetsunma with four heads and twelve arms along with all the associated practices.

76

During a night at Tsurphu, he had a vision of Jetsunma with consort surrounded by thirty-six heroines. The artist Gartön Horpa drew a picture that resembled the deity. Rinpoche said he would give the sadhana to Shönnu and he did.

77

Dusum Khyenpa blessed this sadhana and taught it to others. In a dream one night he saw among the woods three young women with ornaments, who warned him, "Do not explain the profound Dharma to just anyone!" The second and third nights, they also admonished him not to give explanations. Exasperated, they said, "You're not listening!" And so he stopped teaching for a time.

78

At Tsurphu he dreamt that he went to the Five-Peaked Mountain in China where noble Manjushri resides. At the foot of the mountain in a grove with many kinds of trees that sheltered numerous temples, he met Lama Bero. Dusum Khyenpa discussed his meditative experience with him, and they had many other conversations.

79

At Tsurphu, when a few of the great meditators were receiving blessings, he had a clear vision of Sengdeng Nakyi Drölma with a retinue of four.

80

At Tsurphu a geshe, who was leading a group, requested blessings from Dusum Khyenpa. When Rinpoche was making the offerings and chanting the praises, he extended them longer than usual.

When they were finished, Rinpoche said, "I had a vision of Chakrasamvara with sixty-two deities. Did you not see it?"

"How could you see it?" asked the geshe.

"A good experience of samadhi arose," was the reply.

81

He 'dreamt at Tsurphu that he went to the eastern region of a realm in this world. In a rainbow with a carpet of white flowers, he saw Jowo Avalokiteshvara, who gave him a copious amount of medicine pills, saying, "Give these to others and they will benefit."

82

At Tsurphu he had a clear vision of glorious Chakrasamvara with two arms, embraced by his consort and surrounded by four deities.

83

While Tsangpa Tsulseng was receiving an empowerment at Tsurphu, Rinpoche appeared to him as Hevajra with eight faces and sixteen arms. Light shone from his heart and pierced the rows of monks. After leaving the empowerment, the vision continued until Tsangpa Tsulseng fell asleep. Also, when Geshe Yappa Sherin was receiving an empowerment, he saw red Vajra Yogini.

Again at Tsurphu in the summer of the Year of the Dog, on the day of commemorating Gampopa's passing, Rinpoche was sitting in the middle of three hundred ordained members of the Sangha seated in rows. Geshe Sumpa had a vision of him as Hevajra with eight heads and sixteen arms, embraced by his consort. He saw myriad lights radiating from Hevajra's fingers and elsewhere; the tips of these rays penetrated all the monks. He saw visions the whole day long, yet trying to express them would transcend mind's capacity.

84

At Tsurphu while engaged in mantrayana offerings, Dusum Khyenpa had a vision of the mandala of Bhagavan Guhyasamaja.[18]

85

At Tsurphu, while he was engaged in making offerings to her, he had a clear vision of Jetsunma.[19]

86

At Tsurphu he had a vision of glorious Yamantaka with four skull cups and surrounded by twelve deities. He also drew a painting of this yidam deity.

87

While Dusum Khyenpa was at Tsurphu, one of the great meditators at Trewo became sick. He supplicated Rinpoche, who appeared to him. To receive an empowerment from his feet, the meditator thought of prostrating, but Rinpoche said, "That's not necessary. May the obstacle of sickness not come to you." Then he faded away and vanished. There are innumerable stories like this.

88

During the twenty-third night of the snake (or fourth) month, Dusum Khyenpa 'dreamt that within a mass of fire sat a yogi who held an arrow in his right hand and performed all activities with his left. He said:

> If you don't know who I am,
> I am renowned as Saraha.

Rinpoche asked him for a key instruction, and he responded:

> If free of the four extremes, it is the view.
> If free of distraction, it is meditation.
> If free of refuting or proving, it is conduct.
> If free of abandoning or achieving, it is the result.

So saying, he disappeared.

89

One night at Tsurphu Rinpoche dreamt that as he looked out at the border between the south and west, a dragon's roar of thunder from the near sky came rumbling toward him.

In a mass of fire, a yogi holding a long, narrow damaru in his right hand said, "I am Maitripa. All the phenomena of samsara and nirvana can be condensed into two: the afflicted mind and the spontaneously present mind. Furthermore, the afflicted mind is included in the spontaneously present mind." And then he dissolved.

90

On the night of the twenty-seventh of this same snake month, Dusum Khyenpa dreamt that he traveled to Gampo. In his hands, he held one end of a rainbow. As he rolled it up, he followed it along and departed. Rinpoche came to Yangön in Getrang and there met Gampopa. When Rinpoche explained all his previous dreams, his lama said, "Know all phenomena as dreams and rainbows." Then he faded away.

91

Lama Takdeuwa said to him, "You have many emanations that are benefiting living beings. In the world these days, how many are there?"

"It's not certain, but there seem to be four."

"Where are they living?"

"One lives in the monastery of Lama Bero, located on the road along the border of Tibet and Nepal. He has taken birth as Genyen Chökyi Drakpa and benefits beings by teaching the Dharma through signs."

92

"The second one, Bhikshu Geway Lodrö, lives on the far side of Ngari and this side of Kashmir in a city called Surik, where he has built many temples. His previous disciple Tsun Chung died and was reborn in that city. The bhikshu is benefiting a few living beings."

93

"The third one is a yogi who had realized Avalokiteshvara and lives in the south of India without a fixed residence. To some he appears as Avalokiteshvara, while others call him Avalokiteshvara."

94

"The fourth is a realized master who lives in a realm of the world to the east and appears as a king. If he were not its king, he would not be able to tame the kingdom, so he has chosen this way to benefit others."

95

One morning, Dusum Khyenpa was not feeling well. "In last night's dream," he said, "a red young woman came forth from my body and fled. Reflecting on this, I thought that it might be a sign of death, so I emanated a curved knife and brought her back. It is said that among the four signs of dying, Lama Khorowa 'dreamt of three, all of which he was able to reverse. As for myself, I don't know how it will go."

96

On the first day of the tiger (or first) month in the Year of the Ox, Dusum Khyenpa gathered to him a few of the senior monks, including Geshe Tsangpowa, Pöndul, Pön Drakseng, Drakrin, Könchok Gyaltsen, and Na Ünpa. At this time, Rinpoche gave his final words. "All that I possess are the clothes that cover my body and a stone mill for grinding roasted barley. Everything else belongs to the Sangha. The five of ou should take possession of the twenty-five gold sang, the silver and turquoise, silk brocade, dzo, horses, and everything in the kitchen. Use them to benefit the monks who do retreat. After I depart, stay here for one or two years." Pön Drakseng asked, "How long should we stay?"

Rinpoche straightened his body and opened his eyes wide, "At the least, wouldn't it be for one or two years? Furthermore, Shönnu, you stay here for one or two years. Do not lose so much as a single letter from the representations of body, speech, and mind related to my practice. I will also give a command and entrust them all to the Dharma protectors."

97

For three months before that night, many great signs occurred—rainbows, earthquakes, a huge roaring sound, and many others. In particular, going from the night of the second into the third day, earthquakes shuddered continuously and rainbow parasols floated above the monastery. Crowds of dakinis, sounds of damarus, and so forth appeared.

On the third, after breakfast, the monks were allowed to come and see him. Then he said, "Now go outside." Afterward, he straightened his body, sat in vajra posture, and looked for a long time into space. Covering his head with part of his robes, he entered into his final meditation. On the evening of the third day, when the sun and moon came close together, he left for another world realm to benefit beings.

98

At Tsurphu, during the cremation on the tenth day of the month, the people who had gathered observed many different sights. The sun stayed longer than usual, and its rays took the shape of a parasol fasioned of peacock feathers. Dakas and dakinis clad in bone ornaments came into view. It rained flowers. Rainbow parasols floated in tiers above the cremation stupa. The smoke transformed into rainbows in which Rinpoche appeared. Flights of birds circled the rising smoke. The sound of the fire resonated in beautiful melodies, and wild animals gathered to pay their respects. Those not previously engaged in spiritual activity became engaged; those already engaged developed their practice further.

In the cremation stupa Dusum Khyenpa left behind relics for the benefit of others: his heart, which was emptiness and compassion inseparable, his tongue, which had proclaimed the Dharma of different vehicles, and relics of his bodhichitta. Due to his attainment of stability in the creation stage, numerous images of deities also came forth.

99

After Dusum Khyenpa had passed away, most of the monks had dispersed by the winter of the new year. In the spring, those who remained included Geshe Tsangpowa, Sherjung, Könchok Senge, Pön Rinchen Senge, and Pön Drakseng. Entrusted with the care of the main seat, this core group of monks met to discuss the situation. They all thought that Tsurphu was difficult to maintain and hard for people to reach. In general, they also agreed that Chara would be suitable for the main seat because it was in the heart of the region and easily accessible by road.

They asked Gomdar to be the manager and then gathered at Chara. They invited the master artist Tau Rinchen from Gang who was skilled in making reliquary stupas. They also called Geshe Nyale, a master of making earthen stupas. They took on all the work. Geshe Yorpo was put in charge of laying out the foundation for the offering chamber to be erected on top of an existing building.

At that time, Master Sherrin said, "Listen here, you two. Rinpoche turned his thoughts to Tsurphu Monastery and came here from Kampo Nenang. Here he gathered a community of monks and bestowed his final words. Here he passed away and here, too, his body was cremated. During his meditations here, he had many visions of deities and performed numerous empowerments and consecrations. If you leave this blessed land, where would you go?"

Then the teacher and two disciples made a commitment. They would blend ashes from the cremation with milk, perfume, and other precious substances and fashion them into a statue of Dusum Khyenpa. Inside would be placed relics from the Buddha; remains from the Kagyu lamas of the past; relics from the remains of Rinpoche as well as his hair, fingernails, toenails, robes, and so forth. When the statue was completely finished, it would be placed in his former sleeping quarters to inspire wonder and devotion.

So that the ashes and so forth from the cremation would not deteriorate, they wished to build a reliquary stupa. The leaders and disciples discussed this.

"You can find many traditions of stupas all over, but they are not very remarkable."

"Well, then what would be quite special?'

"An earthen one like the Glorious Drepung Stupa. This is what we should build."

It has been said that in this world there are most wondrous representations of body, speech, and mind. One lies in southern India, and it is known as the Glorious Drepung Stupa, a representation of the dharmakaya. It has an umbrella that does not touch the stupa. Four great gods were the sponsors and the artist Vishvakarman made it. Representing the sambhogakaya is the statue of Glorious Vairocana Gangchentso in the outer ocean. It is made of five different jewels, and on the crown of his head is a large water crystal offered by Rahula. The statue itself was created by Vishvakarman. In Bodhgaya is the nirmanakaya representation, a statue imbued with perfume made from a special white sandalwood. Created by Vishvakarman and sponsored by the youngest of three Brahmin brothers, it represents the Buddha at the age of eight and has jewel eyes.

At a later time, the pandita who resided at Drepung Stupa called in an artist from eastern India who painted a great thangka showing the stupa's precise form: the vase section resembling a shrine hall and those parts offered by Nagarjuna—the iron mountains of vajras, the four gates above, and the four great gods. All around this was depicted the life story of Master Nagarjuna. The pandita then carried this thangka to Tibet and gave it to his disciples who were teachers.

Hearing that the thangka was now in the temple erected by Geshe Len, Geshe Namparwa's nephew, who was a teacher, along with others,[20] went to Lhasa to give offerings and make a copy of the thangka. They studied the plastering and the measurements of the stupa from Geshe Namparwa's disciple, Belbu Lotsawa, who had gone to India twice from Lhasa's Tango area. They then returned to Tsurphu.

Previously, Dusum Khyenpa had said, "Here, behind our monastery, build a Drepung Stupa and circumambulate it," so they had the spiritual authority to construct one. In the place where his body had been cremated, they consecrated the ground for this stupa in a ceremony of five stages, and so forth. On that day, there was a great snowfall and the sky was filled with rainbows shaped like parasols, which appeared from that day onward until the stupa was finished.

At the monastery, they meditated on bodhichitta for the humans and nonhumans who create obstacles to virtuous activity. They wore the armor of patience to turn aside the blows of verbal weapons. In order to fulfill the wishes of the precious lama—the essential nature of all the buddhas—Master Sherrin generated bodhichitta and took his measuring stick in hand. After I completed the walls, I finished in ten days the construction of the stupa all the way up to the plinth resting on top of the vase section.[21]

Gyalpo Dorje Drak was called in to do the fine plaster finish, and the work was done in half a month. Looking like a perfect metal casting or bas-relief of the original image, the stupa was completed in twenty-five days, and everyone who saw it said, "Magnificent!"

Within the stupa were relics of the buddhas; a bone of the Tathagata Langpo; leaves and buds from the Bodhi Tree; the earth from the eight great places; and eleven cast-metal statues from Khotan, the foremost of which was an eighteen-inch statue of the glorious Khasarpani. There were many representations of speech, such as three volumes written in gold, and many others. From Rinpoche came his hair, bones, relics, fingernails, toenails, robes, cushion, and footprints. From Kagyu masters of the past came bones, hair, and innumerable other precious objects.

Above the vase section were thirteen levels of vajra wheels. Placed above these, a copper cover made by the expert smith Trochen protected the stupa from rain. The faithful disciple Mutsu Aktsom went to Nepal and brought back a fine gold spire, which was installed.

On the vase section appeared an image of Rinpoche, the size of the span between the tips of a thumb and index finger. When viewed from the right distance, the image appeared to be made of light and created by a master artist. Everyone found it wondrous.

This place, where such an excellent and artistic support for Dharma practice had been created and endowed with blessings, was a field for the accumulation of merit by close and devoted disciples. Therefore, Gomchen Repa took on responsibility for the reliquary stupa that held Rinpoche's heart and tongue.

The two bhikshus Rongpa (uncle and nephew) along with other monks and the yogi practitioner Gompa Repa along with other yogis had tremendous loyalty to the main seat of Tsurphu and kept their minds stable and focused. These great leonine meditators concentrated on practice and rested evenly in one-pointed meditative concentration. All of them gathered together and with immense devotion stayed at Tsurphu.

Twenty-one years after the stupa was built, the glory of living beings, the protector Tsangpowa, was living in

Minyak. He repeatedly paid his respects to this main seat of Tsurphu, which resembles Bodhgaya. Tsangpowa offered inconceivably precious articles, such as the representations of body, speech, and mind along with the five varieties of jewels and silk brocades. In particular, he gave a coating mixed with gold to the Drepung Stupa and provided all that was needed for the task, including the artisans who were sent from Minyak Gha.

In order to fulfill all their intentions, Geshe Shenshi Tönshe and Gompa Dorje Jangchup sponsored the care of the artisans, and the kind-hearted Gompa Köntsul assumed the role of manager. The one who did the work on the stupa was a close attendant of Rinpoche named Shönnu, generally skilled in the various arts and particularly adept at building this kind of stupas. Once the stupa was well prepared, the artisans from Mashar offered the coating mixed with gold.

All the monks living at the main seat, old and young alike, were inspired by faith and joyous diligence. The inside of the stupa was spacious like an infinite palace; the four gates had their protectors; and the four kings resided in their abodes on the terraces. It was built eight armspans around with sides of equal length.[22] Once the walls were finished, from Dechen Sölnak Tangpoche they called a talented youth who was very skilled in plastering, a shining example of his craft. The plaster was made from silver, and the color shone silver as well. It was all finished in two years.

Functioning as an ornamental shield, a curved roof of azure blue tiles crafted by a skilled artisan was placed above the stupa to protect it from rain. For the top of the stupa,

Chungpo Josey sent a considerable amount of funds to a Nepalese craftsperson to make a spire. It was brought to Tsurphu from far away and placed on the center of the stupa, making it a radiant place at the monastery.

Everyone who saw the stupa, knowledgeable and ordinary alike, said that this great work of art was most excellent. Like a glorious banner, its fame pervaded all the countries under the sun. It became the template for all those building stupas from up in Balpo Dobikpa down to Minyak Gha. Disciples and patrons came from all directions to pay their respects and make offerings. Afterward, when they supplicated, all their goals, both relative and ultimate, were accomplished just as they had wished. It has become a great reliquary stupa, a precious wish-fulfilling gem, providing everything needed and wished for as long as the Buddha's teachings remain.

100

Rinpoche was asked, "After this life, where will you benefit others?"

"In the northeast of Uddiyana to the west of India," he replied, "there is a land known as Kartika. I will take birth there as the yogi Dharmasiddhi, who will benefit living beings and meet Lama Gampopa."

101

"After that," he said, "I will take birth in Central Tibet in the seven places of practice in Lhodrak. I will take birth for the sake of one disciple and also benefit others. I will not stay long.

102

"In Murupa of southern India, I will be born in a place of the dakinis called Kongka. In that area, there is a city called Patala where the patron Gönpawa will take birth as a king and benefit many people who have taken the wrong path."

103

When Dusum Khyenpa was staying at Tsurphu, an offering was arranged by some forty senior great meditators, led by Master Könchok Senge.

He asked Rinpoche, "In the future, when the Lord of Dharma has become fully and perfectly awakened, who will be in the first retinue to gather around you?"

"In the future, there will be four people who will come together as the first retinue. One is the yogi Mitra Jogi, residing in the temple called Lokeshwara Vihara. Then another is Geway Lodrö, living in the west of Ngari and greatly benefiting others. There will also be the Dharma king of Minyak's lama, Yarlungpa, who is also called Gyabebum Rimo and is famous as Gya Bodhisattva. The final one is the Geshe Könchok Senge, who is you." He recounted many other amazing stories.

Though Dusum Khyenpa never named the buddha he would become, Lama Tsalpa said, "There are many prophecies predicting that the great, glorious one of Tsurphu will be the buddha after Maitreya and known as the Buddha Senge Dra.

104

Rinpoche said, "Master Sherap Jangchup lives on Bird Foot Mountain and benefits many."

105

"Master Gomtsul will be born in the country of Kongka in the south of India. There he will convert a non-Buddhist king and benefit many living beings."

106

"Gampopa Rinpoche has been born in the city of Padmini in the region of India known as Karnapa, located between India and Kashmir. Named Shantivarman, sometimes he appears as a fully ordained monk and sometimes as a yogi. Through numerous activities, he benefits living beings. About forty disciples have taken birth and reside near him."

107

"Gampopa has three emanations. In the western pure land called Placed in Bliss, he benefits millions of living beings as Bodhisattva Drime Drakpa. In Ornamented by Ten Million Pearls, located in an eastern realm of the world, he has the name of Bodhisattva Drime Dawa and works there for the benefit of beings."

108

"In the city of Padmini, Gampopa was born and passed away. Taking birth again in a realm of the worlds above, he has become fully and perfectly enlightened as Ashoka Aja."

For his personal practice, Shanshi Tönshe had a thangka painted with a perfect image of the Protector of Beings, Dusum Khyenpa, surrounded by one hundred and eight pictures from his life. Master Josey saw it and was delighted. He said that a similar narrative should be put into words. Familiar with the life story, the attendant Bhikshu Kumara Ratnabodhi, a monk from the merchant caste, composed this at the main seat of Tsurphu.

Dharma Talks

Advice for Great Meditators

I prostrate to the activity of all the buddhas of the three times: the precious guru who instills faith in all beings through the nine moods of dance; who inspires, ripens, and liberates them; who purifies their faults and perfects their qualities; who skillfully cares for all sentient beings with great compassion.

In the words of the precious Lord of Dharma:

In all of the scriptures taught by the completely perfect Buddha Shakyamuni, there is nothing he taught that is not a method to tame the mind. It is extremely important to give advice to and watch your own mind.

All of us great meditators should not chitchat. Doing that increases our greed and hatred so much that eventually our afflictions will get stronger than an ordinary person's. There is no benefit to spending a night greedy or angry and then saying, "My mind was dull last night and I could not meditate." It would be difficult to become a great meditator doing that.

The thought that we should practice Dharma comes to everybody, but it won't help us a whit on its own. We need to completely cast away all our immediate affairs and practice as if we were in retreat from this day onward. There's no spare time in life. There's no need for us great meditators to try to do one thing after another—that's what all those learned people do. If something helps the mind, it is Dharma practice. Since I am a lama, I give whatever advice will help your mind.

If you feel from the bottom of your heart that you must practice Dharma, it is important to continually watch your mind. Since we are in the mahayana, we must especially treasure loving-kindness and compassion. Since all positive qualities arise due to the lama, it is important for us to be continually devoted at all times, to make our mindfulness taut, and to moisten our minds over and over without being distracted. Then what we call wisdom will definitely come from within.

Instead of studying or reading books, the only thing we meditators should do is meditate without distraction. But if beginners lack adversary that is spiritual training, they won't know how to practice.[23] Their bodies, speech, and minds will slip back into the ordinary. Therefore they should follow a regimen of spiritual training without ever lapsing.

According to some scriptures and spiritual instructions, it does not matter whether you start at dawn or in the evening. Those for whom phlegm is predominant should start at dawn because the mind is clearer then. Those for whom wind is predominant should begin in the evening, as the mind is duller then.

In terms of beginning in the evening, first develop the certainty of the three individuals,[24] starting from death and impermanence up to loving-kindness and compassion. Make whatever torma offering you know, as this gathers the accumulations and dispels obstacles. Visualize the buddhas and bodhisattvas clearly in the sky before you and do the seven branches. Offer a mandala and recite the hundred syllables,[25] as these are important. Then wash up, blow your nose, and take care of anything that might become an obstacle to your spiritual training. Next make yourself comfortable, meditate on bodhichitta, and meditate on the creation and completion phases in union. It is important to be undistracted without lapsing into torpor or agitation. Then when you want to stop your meditation, dedicate it to the benefit of sentient beings. As long as we are in the Desire realm and have brains in our heads, sleep will come, so sleep for a long session at night in order to refresh your faculties for the benefit of sentient beings. However, it is important to tell yourself that you will get up early. That itself is spiritual training.

Then get up early in the morning, go to the bathroom, and so forth. Wash up, or at least rinse your mouth and blow your nose. Develop the resolve to benefit all sentient beings. Meditate on creation and completion in union. When it is time for breakfast, offer the seven branches to the Jewels. Then after breakfast, offer mandalas and supplicate the lamas, yidams, dakas, and dakinis. Do as many hundred-syllable mantras as you can. Once again, meditate on creation and completion in union without distraction according to the lama's instructions. Do not let yourself become torpid or agitated. At lunchtime, do the seven branches. When lunch is finished, perform the blessings of the body, speech, and mind. To dispel drowsiness, circumambulate. Additionally, recite profound sutras, make tormas or tsatsas, and do whatever positive activities are appropriate.

If you fail to do this and place your hopes in the view, nothing will happen. One wing is not enough for a bird in the sky; one leg is not enough for a human being on the ground. It is critical to never be distracted from the union of means and wisdom.

You must pacify your thoughts in order to become a completely perfect buddha free of any conceptual elaboration, to achieve the indivisibility of the expanse and pristine wisdom. You must meditate to still your thoughts from their roots. Through the wisdom born of meditation, you will recognize the thought itself as the mind of the Buddha, the dharmakaya. It does not work to use another concept from listening and contemplating as an antidote for a thought that needs to be discarded. That is just like taking as a remedy for fever medicines that produce heat, such as beer mixed with molasses—they won't prevent death or cure illness.

You might have the final, ultimate view from listening and contemplating, but it is just a horse's tail in comparison to realization—there's nothing exalted about it. It's empty. It is not enough to cast aside all the composite virtue you have done, say you don't need meditation, and place your hope in a high view. In the entire great middle way, there is no thinking, "It is not empty," or "The essence of all phenomena is not empty." Without meditating, the mind itself won't be able to recognize anything. The master and spiritual friend Tölungpa Gya once said, "I have that ultimate view, but I need a way to hold the mind." He recounted how he had heard of a lama named Durtröpa in Nepal who was a siddha, and how he fell ill along the way to meet him.

Then, without having meditated, all these great meditators say, "I don't need anything. There's no way a thought can hurt me." This assumption doesn't work at all. That is the momentary thought that will make us take birth in samsara. It won't get us anywhere. Even a buddha can't do anything with an aroused goat who has not eliminated thoughts and afflictions.

If we go through complete and thorough spiritual training, eventually we will be so familiarized with it that we will be able to do any meditation without ever lapsing. Only then will experience and realization come. Only then will thoughts be unable to harm us. "The thought cannot harm us" means that the thought itself subsides on its own, like clouds clearing from the sky or ice melting into a lake, so that there's no way it can arise. That is what we need. When thoughts arise in their ordinary way, that itself is the harm.

Why do we need all this? At some point we must die. If when we died we became nothing, that would be fine. But we must be reborn. If we commit the ten nonvirtues, we will be born in the lower realms, which are unbearable. Even if we take birth in the higher realms through the ten virtues, even in the high realms there is nothing other than suffering—no happiness, no friends or family. The nature of samsara is suffering. To abandon that nature of suffering, we need to use this precious human body with its leisures and resources to cut the ties to samsara. Now we have met a true spiritual friend who has the precious spiritual instructions from an unbroken lineage of experience and realization. These instructions have not been tainted by words and conventions or diluted like milk for sale. We have the fortune to hear them. At this time when we have some slight inclination to do Dharma, we need to put aside all our affairs and all our strategies to avoid upsetting others. We need to make an effort from today. I ask you to please keep this in mind.

ITHI

Four Things That Are Important for Practice

I prostrate to the precious spiritual friend. In Rinpoche's words:

These four things are important for practice: Always contemplate death. Assess the karma you have accumulated. Offer to the Three Jewels. Meditate on the nondual essence. There are no Dharma practices that are not contained within these four.

As for the first, my lama Gampopa said that the contemplation of death is important in the beginning. Remember that those who are older than you die. The young and those in the prime of life die. Townspeople and neighbors die. Everyone must die. When we die, our possessions, fame, and so forth will not help at all. They cannot go with us.

> Alas, the afflicted in this world
> Do not like impermanence.
> Even these glorious *kumuda* blossoms[26]
> Will become a mere memory.

As this says, understand that we will need to leave everything in this life behind and go. Although we need it at death, the Dharma is rare. Understanding this causes us to enter the

Dharma in the beginning.

It is important in the middle: The time of death is unknown, as *The Way of the Bodhisattva* says:

> If I should perish soon and die
> Without purifying my misdeeds,
> How could I liberate myself?
> I ask that you protect me swiftly.

Since we do not know when we will die, we should feel that we do not have the leisure to sit down and put our feet up. This spurs us to engage in the Dharma.

Dharma is important in the end. It has been said that "death is transcendent wisdom" and that "the word death is ultimate truth." It is also said that "death is the dharmakaya." You might think that meditating on death is just a Dharma of the foundation vehicle. However, it is said that it is more important to meditate on death than on either the paramitas or the tantras.

You might wonder whether we will become nothing when we die, as the non-Buddhist Charvaka school says. We will not become nothing. The second thing is to assess the karma you have accumulated. We must take birth according to our karma. If we have performed the ten unvirtuous actions primarily out of hatred, we will be born in hell, where there are the unbearable sufferings of heat and cold, of being cooked, cut, chopped, sliced, burned, and so forth. Now we cannot stand it if a spark falls on our body or if we have to spend a single day outside without clothes and end up sneezing. In order to avoid the suffering of hell, we need to eliminate its cause, so it is important that we do not perform the ten nonvirtues out of hatred, even at the cost of our own life.

If we do not give up hatred and anger, even in terms of the common going for refuge, we will lack the four traits of spiritual training.[27] In terms of being bodhisattvas, we need consider all sentient beings as our mothers and meditate on loving-kindness, but hatred and loving-kindness cannot coexist. Hatred also easily destroys the virtue accumulated over thousands of aeons. In terms of the secret mantra, we need to meditate on the inhabitants of the world as deities. But if we have hatred toward them, there is no way we can see the face of the yidam deity. If the elimination of hatred is possible, it comes from what is called the samadhi of great loving-kindness. But when you get right down to it, that samadhi is what we call understanding that hatred has no reality.

If we commit the ten nonvirtues primarily through desire, we will be born as hungry ghosts, and we will not even hear about food or drink. If we should happen to see food, it would be protected by five hundred guards with hammers. There would be no way to bear the suffering from hunger and thirst. Now we start to turn green and fade if we go even a day without food. Thus it is important to give up desire.

Even in this life, covetousness destroys our hopes. We will not achieve anything. We will not accomplish any tasks or attain wealth, prosperity, or what we want. We will end up breaking the samaya and the vows to which we must commit. If great meditators do not view desire as a fault, they will be driven by sensory pleasures, their minds unable to rest within for even an instant. The samadhi of the treasury of space is simply the complete pacification of desires.

If we commit the ten nonvirtues primarily through delusion, we will be born as animals. In the outer oceans, there are animals the size of the dregs from brewing beer who are eaten when enormous animals open their mouths. With this and infinite other sufferings, there is not even an instant of happiness. Horses, cows, and the like are the happiest—they are in the heavens of the animal realms. But they have the *duḥkha*[28] of being driven into pens at slaughterhouses. Thus it is important to give up committing the ten nonvirtues primarily out of delusion. If that were possible without giving up delusion:

> If there were a self, we'd know another.
> Grasping at self and other brings
> Clinging and hatred. In connection
> With these two, all wrongs arise.

Since the root of all wrongdoing is delusion, it is important to eliminate it. What eliminates it is the wisdom of listening, contemplating, and meditating. If you are going to listen, listen to the mahayana Dharma. If your are going to contemplate, contemplate the mahayana Dharma. If you are going to meditate, you must meditate on the mahayana Dharma: listening and contemplating the Dharma of the foundation vehicle is like boxing yourself into a corner. If the elimination of delusion is possible, it is called the samadhi of great luminosity or the pacification of delusion.

Therefore, it is said that it is important to give up the ten nonvirtues motivated by the three poisons. Even if we are born as gods or humans through the ten virtuous actions, samsara is by nature suffering. Other than that, there are no joys, friends, or relatives.

> Even if you are born as Great Indra himself,
> By force of karma, you will become a slave again.

You might wonder what we need to do to give up samsara, whose nature is suffering, and develop nirvana within our beings. The third thing, offering to the Three Jewels, means you must gather the accumulations. As it is said, "If you want merit, offer to the Tathagata." We need to make offerings to the Three Jewels.

The best offering is the offering of practice. In terms of the transcendences, this is the conduct of the six transcendences and the four means of nurturing disciples. In terms of secret mantra, it is doing creation and completion meditation for four sessions and so forth. The middling offering is the offering of the body. Sweeping paths and so forth is said to be offering your body to the lama and the Three Jewels. The least offering is to arrange material offerings. Because of such offerings:

> Whatever aspiration someone makes,
> It will become just so.

As this says, all the aspirations you make will be fulfilled. There is no difference between this and purifying the winds and mind in the secret mantra in order to perform *phowa*. Additionally, bodhichitta initially arises because of gathering merit in relation to the Jewels.

You might wonder whether the accumulation of merit

alone is enough to achieve nirvana. The fourth thing is to meditate on the nondual nature. We need the accumulation of wisdom—meditation on emptiness.

> The Sage taught all these branches
> For the sake of wisdom.

Also:

> By realizing emptiness you'll be liberated;
> Other meditations are for that sake.

Making offerings to the Three Jewels and so forth are methods to recognize emptiness; they are the provisional meaning. But just saying everything is empty does not help. It does not matter whether you want the north side of a boulder to be empty or not. Empty space has always been empty, but that doesn't help. We need to recognize that our own minds are emptiness.

> They want to attain that and conquer suffering
> But wander pointlessly in the ordinary.

We need to realize mind, and if we realize mind, that is pristine wisdom, so it is buddha. Thus it is said, "Do not look for buddha elsewhere." But that is also emptiness, as is said:

> My primordially unborn mind
> Has the characteristic of emptiness.

Well then, you wonder, what is the spiritual advice to realize this?

In this, there's nothing to remove
Nor anything at all to add.
Looking authentically at the authentic
And seeing authentically is liberation.

Additionally:

When neither thing nor nothing
Is present before the mind,
As there is no other aspect,
Without support, it's total peace.

In these and other quotations, the meditation instruction is to rest in the state of the fresh, unaltered mind itself without any reference. That alone will bring the initial union of tranquillity and insight. Instead of doing that, you could take the understanding that looks for emptiness outside through conceptual discernment of the view and make the experience of stagnant tranquillity into meditation. But this will never bring you any realization and experience or the union of tranquillity and insight. Thus you must rest in the state of awareness itself and recognize from within awareness itself. You understand it is not necessary to look elsewhere with your intellect and that there is no basis, so there is no fear of the three deviations.[29] Because you are not resting the mind outside or losing yourself to an object of reference, there is no fear of the four strayings.[30] That alone is freedom from all views and assertions. Realizing mind, your meditation is free of anything to identify, and it transcends any focus or thing that focuses. Your conduct is free of all giving up and taking up. Your view, meditation, and conduct all become of one taste. The three poisons no longer have any basis, so you can enter the ultimate samadhis such as the samadhi of great loving-kindness. Generally, as the precious lama said:

> By the method, resting in the state of awareness,
> Wisdom is recognized within awareness.
> All is liberated in the state of awareness.
> You become learned in all views and knowledge.

Therefore, "meditate on the nondual" means that meditating on mind is important.

But what is necessary for these four things?

> You may perfect all qualities,
> Yet without a lama, there is no end to existence.

And:

> Until you attain perfect buddhahood, please the spiritual friend.

And:

> "All the qualities of the Buddha depend upon the spiritual friend,"
> Said the Victor, who has the supreme qualities.

A lama is important, but following just any lama does not help. The lama should be someone engaged in the activity of all buddhas of the three times. You should feel blessings just by seeing their body and so forth. In the beginning, the lama should be experienced in the methods of how to bring to rest a mind that will not rest and how to recognize the samadhi of resting. You should rely upon such a lama who has experience and realization.

Well then, how should you follow them? Avoid being disrespectful. Attend to them respectfully with your body, speech, and mind. To be respectful with your body, avoid sitting in the lama's presence with your legs stretched out, not prostrating when the lama arrives, not standing up, and so forth.

Sit on a low seat,
Give rise to the glory of being tamed.
Look with a joyful eye.
Just as the earth is like a seat,
When performing the lama's activity,
Give up a discouraged, weary attitude.
Have faith and sincerity like a river's current.

As this says, follow the lama with great respect. Respectfulness of speech means that you should give up talk of business, fighting, and sex as well as other impure speech that is motivated by the three poisons. Speak respectful and worthy words such as asking Dharma questions and so forth.

Disrespect of mind is to view the lama as having faults. The lama is a mirror of the student, so the lama appears to have whatever traits are actually present in your own being. If you say that the lama is an ill-tempered, stingy, or argumentative person who craves wealth or does not teach Dharma—or to sum it up, if instead of thinking about the lama's qualities you think about their faults—that is disrespect. If you act in such a manner, there will be no way to extricate yourself from samsara. It is said with regard to this, "Achievement follows the master." It is important to avoid disrespecting the lama. Therefore, show the lama respect. View all their actions as the buddhas' activity. If you see them in that way, all illness and harm will subside. All qualities will arise in your being as if you were a vase being filled to the brim. It is said that you need what will be necessary for you when you lie on your deathbed. I ask you to please keep this in mind.

Impediments to Secret Mantra Meditation Practice

I prostrate to the precious guru. In Rinpoche's words:

When you do true meditation practice of the secret mantra, being attached and imagining you have qualities are the greatest demons. When Nagarjuna saw the truth of the first bodhisattva level, he did Yakshini practice but was unable to achieve anything. Master Nagabodhi saw that Nagarjuna was attached to a clay vase that looked like a raven's eye, so Nagabodhi smashed it. Nagarjuna was then able to accomplish Yakshini practice. A pile of hay across from his retreat house then transformed and appeared as jewels and food, and Yakshini revealed herself in her own form. Nagarjuna was annoyed with her, but Yakshini said, "I was here from the beginning, but you were too attached to that clay vase."

Then Nagarjuna clung to four different conceits. He said to himself, "There is no one senior to me in the vows—I'm five hundred years old. There is no one with more knowledge than I have—there's not a single scripture I don't know. There is no one with greater powers than I have—I know how to milk the wish-fulfilling cow and perform alchemy to create gold. There is no one more compassionate than I am—I benefit beings in many different ways."

Then Nagarjuna went to a town in India, where he met a bhikshu. "How long have you held your vows?" he asked the bhikshu. "I took vows during the time of Buddha Kashyapa," replied the bhikshu, shattering Nagarjuna's first conceit. Then when he went to the land of the nagas, he met a dakini who could not count how many scriptures she knew, shattering another of his conceits. He then went somewhere else and his foot got stuck in vajra mud. It was freed by him praying to Lady Tara, and another conceit was shattered. Then he went to a place where there was the corpse of a dead dog that stank so much that he could not come near it. But there was an old beggar who removed the maggots from the dog, cut off a piece of his own flesh, and fed it to the maggots. Nagarjuna thought, "I don't have as much compassion as that old beggar," and his conceit was shattered. Only then did any of the precious qualities arise within his mind.

Once there was a bodhisattva named Master Chandradvaja. He had such good samadhi that he did not even sense it when a bird landed on his head, but he was overcome by pride. One night he had a dream of a radiant lay person, who said, "Pride has got the better of someone like that. For you to do true meditation, follow the meditation of one hundred and eight masters. Teach meditation to one hundred and eight students. Rebuild one hundred and eight ruined monasteries. Build one hundred and eight stupas. Lead one hundred and eight bhikshus to teach Dharma. Teach Dharma in one hundred and eight prisons." The master thought about this: "If I don't have enough for my own food and clothing, how can I rebuild temples and all that?"

"It is not necessary to fear what appears in one night's dream," replied the lay man. "Rebuild my Kharsapani temple. If you clean and fix up the temple, I will offer food and money." The man's body produced abundance, and there was inexhaustible wealth. With what remained, Chandradvaja provided sustenance for one thousand monastics, and what was left over was enough for only seventy-five prisoners in one jail, it was said.

In general, do not place great hopes in gods or dreams. There is a danger that doing so would become an obstacle; there is a danger you would cling to the sight of them. Only when you can seal experiences with the stamp of no hope and no fear will accomplishment come. Imagining you have some slight qualities becomes a blockage on the path, it is said. If qualities don't develop, it is not appropriate to resent merit. If you meet a good lama, receive excellent instructions, and put them into practice, that is greater merit. Greater wealth does not make greater merit. The king of the nagas has a precious jewel, but what good does it do? He is an animal. Everyone else who is headed for lower realms is like that.

Having the fortune to practice Dharma in these times is even rarer than an *udumwara* flower.[31] Animals have bright clarity in their minds but are in a wretched state due to the power of their karma. Whether people have good practice or bad, they will come to die, enter the bardo, and take their next birth. If your practice is bad now, even though you may have many instructions, they won't help. It's like reading about medical treatment. We do not know when death will come. There is no end to the young people who die thinking they will never die. If there is a fight, people in their prime die in an instant. You might think you won't die from old age, but there is no one left. At the time of death, when your life is finished, even the Buddha coming will not help, so I ask you to try hard now.

If you don't know your acts are confused, you can't stop them. There is conceptual and nonconceptual confusion. Listening and contemplating can take care of conceptual confusion, but they cannot take care of nonconceptual confusion. You might understand that there is no nature, but that cannot stop confusion. When you press your eyeballs, you understand that the mountain and its appearance are not double and that the appearance does not inherently exist, but until you stop pressing, you cannot stop them from appearing double. Alternatively, someone with cataracts can't heal them on their own. Just as you need a good doctor who uses medicine to heal cataracts, you must meditate. Therefore it is said meditation is a critical point.

When you lie on your deathbed and eat your final meal, nothing other than having meditated will help, so I ask you to put aside all your pursuits and meditate.

ITHI

The Elements of the Path to Achieve Enlightenment

NAMO GURU. *In Rinpoche's words*:

It is said that these four qualities are important for individuals who want to achieve unexcelled enlightenment:

> With conduct, listening, contemplation,
> Completely train in meditation.

First, discipline is important:

> That is why the Teacher lauded discipline.
> Those with discipline will meet the buddhas when
> they appear.

Also:

> Like the earth for beings who move or who do not,
> Discipline is the basis for all qualities.

You will have no regrets if you keep pure discipline. Thus it is a cause for the development of superior samadhi.

Secondly, listening is important:

> Listening is the great torch that dispels the darkness of ignorance.
> It is the friend who never deserts you in times of distress.
> It is the supreme jewel that thieves and the like cannot steal.
> It is the best of friends when you meet high and good people.

Also:

> You turn away from misdeeds through listening.
> You give up the meaningless through listening.
> You learn the specifics of Dharma through listening.
> You achieve nirvana through listening.

As these and others say, listening is important.

> It is a joy for those who've listened much
> To stay within the forest as life passes.
> If you wish to gain the qualities of a buddha,
> Follow a person who has listened much.
> Respect virtue as your abbot, and
> You will quickly accomplish buddhahood.

Thirdly, on top of that, the wisdom from contemplation is also important. Without contemplation, you are like a leaky pot—what you have listened to goes to waste:

> Like water in a leaky vase,
> It does not stay in memory.

As this says, you must contemplate. Contemplation suppresses the afflictions.

However, if you do not meditate, it does not help. From *The Buddha Avatamsaka Sutra*:

> For instance, just as ships at sea
> Free many beings yet remain
> Themselves in the midst of the water,
> Such is Dharma without meditation.
>
> For instance, just as a blind artist
> Amidst the six assemblies draws
> Though he can't see when on his own,
> Such is Dharma without meditation.
>
> For instance, as a deaf musician
> Amidst the six assemblies plays
> Though he can't hear when on his own,
> Such is Dharma without meditation.

Well then, you wonder, how should you meditate? The meditation should be the union of tranquillity and insight.

> Know that when fully joined with shamatha,
> Insight eradicates afflictions.
> Seek shamatha at first, and then with joy
> Achieve detachment from the world.

In the beginning, it is important to settle the mind that won't stay. In the middle, it is important that it rest stably. In the end, the instructions for enhancing that stability are important. Once the mind rests in a superior way, the reflection of the moon of insight will appear in the clear lake of shamatha.

Regarding the instructions for developing insight:

> If you don't know this secret of the mind…

And:

> In this, there's nothing to remove
> Nor anything at all to add.
> Looking authentically at the authentic
> And seeing authentically is liberation.

Also:

> Unobscured by thought and consciousness
> Is the characteristic of emptiness.

Also:

> If with this mind that is like space
> You do meditation that is like space
> On dharmas that are like space,
> You will become awakened like space.

Also:

If you realize mind, that is buddha, so do not search for buddhahood elsewhere.

Thus develop insight.
When insight has developed, from *The Vajra Cutter*:

Whoever sees me as a form
Or knows me as a sound
Has entered into the wrong path:
That person does not see me.
The dharmakaya of the guides,
The dharmata cannot be known—
These cannot be cognized.

Also from the Prajnaparamita:

Whoever sees no forms and also sees no feelings,
Who sees no conceptions and no volition,
Who sees no consciousness, no mind, no intellect,
Is one who sees the Dharma, the Tathagata has taught.

Atisha also said, "There's no seeing anything to see in it."

However, Dharma never comes without remembering death. Thus meditating on death itself is a profound point. When you lie on your deathbed, eat your last meal, and say, "Hahhh..." it is important to have no regrets.

May those with faith and intelligence
Practice the precious exalted instructions
That heal the illnesses of the fortunate
And extract the essence of the nectar of deathlessness.

ITHI

Six Things for Quickly Achieving Enlightenment

I prostrate to the precious lama. In the words of the precious master:

Those who wish to achieve unexcelled buddhahood in one lifetime and one body need to have six things, it is said:

> Faith, wisdom, compassion,
> Meeting the lama, requesting Dharma,
> And effort in accomplishing its purpose.

Among these, faith is important at the beginning:

> Good qualities will not arise
> In people who do not have faith,
> Just as green shoots will never grow
> From seeds that fire has burnt.

This explains the many detriments of lacking faith. As far as the benefits of faith, from *The Summary of All Trainings:*

> After stabilizing the root, faith,
> Fix your mind on enlightenment.

It is explained to be the root of all traits that are good qualities.

> The ultimate of the self-arisen[32]
> Is realized only through faith.
> Those with no eyes can never see
> The brilliant orb of the sun.

As this says, the ultimate nature, the unborn meaning, can only be realized by those who have superior faith. From *The Gandavyuha Sutra*:

> Faith is the treasure, the jewel, and the best foot.
> Like a hand, it is the basis for gathering virtue.
> It guards and develops every quality.
> Faith comes first; it is like a mother giving birth.
> Faith makes the tree of enlightenment grow.

I have often explained this properly to the lay people in the area. Scholars explain that there are many different types of faith, such as faith in what is to be known, the four truths; faith in the result, the three kayas; faith in karma, cause, and result; and faith in the support, the Three Jewels. However, it is said that there is none that is not included in the three faiths: the faith of wishing, sincere faith, and the faith of believing. Thus it is important to have faith.

However, even if you have faith, nothing will happen without wisdom, so wisdom is extremely important. Scholars talk about those with dull faculties who follow faith. If you lack wisdom, then even if you want to teach Dharma, you cannot. Even thinking, "This is the unmistaken thing to do" would be difficult, it seems. Fake spiritual teachers would also have no difficulty deceiving you, it is said. Therefore, Master Shantideva said:

> The Sage taught all these branches
> For the sake of wisdom.

The dhyanas and diligence are all explained to be causes that produce wisdom.

> Therefore those who wish to quell
> Their sufferings should develop wisdom.

This says that wisdom is important for those who wish to quell the suffering of samsara. From the *Paramitas:*

> Without wisdom, these five eyeless paramitas
> Have no guide, so they cannot reach enlightenment.
> When they are completely imbued with wisdom,
> They have found an eye and gain the name.

Any virtue you do that is not imbued with wisdom is like a person blind since birth who has no guide—it cannot become a cause for enlightenment. It cannot even be given the name "transcendent," it is explained. But when imbued with the wisdom of emptiness, anything you do becomes the path to enlightenment—it is said that even giving a crumb to an old dog can become transcendent generosity. Therefore, wisdom is crucial. But just any old wisdom won't get you anywhere. You must recognize the afflictions through the wisdom of listening. You must suppress the afflictions with the wisdom of contemplating. And you must eliminate the afflictions from their root with the wisdom of meditating.

You might have great wisdom, but without compassion, it will not help. Thus compassion is important. The White Lotus of True Dharma says, "There is one quality that, if you have it, will place all qualities in the palm of your hand. What is it? It is great compassion." If someone has a head, they can live. Similarly, if someone has compassion, they can have unexcelled enlightenment. *The King of Samadhi Sutra* states:

> He asked, "Can one achieve unexcelled enlightenment with one quality?"
> "There is unexcelled awakening if you have one quality," replied the Buddha." It is this: great compassion."

Therefore, we need great compassion and wisdom that are linked together. The vehicle of the transcendences explains that we need means and wisdom that are linked together. *The Sutra of Gayagori* says, "Means without wisdom is bondage. Wisdom without means is also bondage." Thus it is important to have means and wisdom that are connected. The meaning of the explanations in the secret mantra that creation and completion must never be separated is that if either one of the two is not present, you will not achieve unexcelled enlightenment—it is like a bird with one wing cut off, it is said.

You may have all three of those qualities, but if you do not meet a lama who can guide you on the path, they do not help.

Even if you perfect all qualities,
There's no end to existence without a lama.
Without a ferryman a boat
Cannot get to the other side.

As this says, it is important to meet a genuine lama.

No one at all should reject the great.
Serve the spiritual friend in a subdued manner.
When close to them, their qualities and tameness
Will rub off on you, even without being specifically cultivated.

That explains that we need to follow a genuine lama. Regarding the characteristics of the lama:

The friend is subdued, peaceful, and fully pacified.
They strive for higher qualities and are rich in scriptures.
They've fully realized suchness and are eloquent.
Their nature is loving. Follow them without discouragement.

The Ornament of the Sutras explains:

Know that they who have seen the truth—
The eloquent, affectionate,
Undaunted noble beings—are great.

In the words of Master Shantideva:

Even if it should cost your life
Never abandon the spiritual friend

Who holds the bodhisattva conduct
And is learned in the mahayana.

There is not a single scripture in the secret mantra or the prajnaparamita that does not speak of the characteristics of a lama. In Gampopa's words, "You need someone who has cut the ties of dependence on this life, who can guide others on the path through great wisdom, and who, because of great compassion, does not forsake their students."

First, lamas who are dependent upon this life are suspicious of students who serve them and so forth, but they won't teach instructions to those who do not. They make this life as long in length and wide in breadth as they can, performing ever more wicked acts out of greed and hatred. Their students serve the master and commit more and more wrongdoing. If things go wrong, it is not difficult for oxen that are yoked together to fall into a chasm. Therefore you need a master who has cut the ties of dependence to this life.

However, without wisdom, a master will not know how to teach Dharma that fits the students' minds. In order to benefit beings who have many different inclinations, the master needs to teach step by step the instructions that match the students' intelligence. It is also said:

If they do not become learned in the five areas of knowledge,
Even the supreme noble beings will not achieve omniscience.

Lord Atisha said:

> In this brief, momentary life of ours, we do not have the leisure to hear many treatises on non-Buddhist subjects such as grammar. We don't have the leisure to study them. The many treatises on Buddhist topics are what are important.

When you ask a lama for a Dharma teaching, it does not work if they say, "I don't know." Therefore you need someone who can guide others on the path through their great wisdom.

But if they lack compassion, at times when they experience the slightest suffering, they will think that they are unable to care for the people around them and get discouraged. When you have to benefit many contentious sentient beings, it is quite possible that the moment you try to nurture them with Dharma, they will respond with many unkind words. If you lack compassion, it is possible that you might think, "Even though I've given them Dharma and worked hard for them, these dunces won't listen," and then you might want to give up on them. If you have little compassion, it is possible that you won't do anything at all to care for your students when they experience suffering. Therefore the lama must feel such great compassion that even at the cost of their own life, they will do anything to prevent the students who place their trust in them from going to the lower realms.

Yet even if you follow such a genuine lama, it does no good unless you request the precious instructions. Dogs, horses, and other animals associate with the lama, but it does not help them. Merely serving the lama for a million years will not help. You must request the precious instructions that have not been muddled. They must not be like milk diluted for sale at market time. They must be not mixed with too many words and expressions. You need the words with blessings that have passed from one ear to the next.

However, if you do not practice appropriately, it is as if those instructions were confined to a notebook; they will not help you.

> Does merely reading of medical treatment
> Bring benefit to the sick?

Reading about medical treatment does not help; you must prepare the medicines and take them. Similarly, just having instructions is not enough; you must practice them. The Bhagavan Buddha said:

> I have explained to you the path
> That cuts the pangs of suffering.
> The Tathagata is the one who teaches;
> You yourselves must practice.

It is said that receiving all the explanations of many instructions is no different from music to a deaf person. It is no different from dying of starvation in the midst of limitless food and wealth—the fault is not being able to eat. Having the instructions is not enough—practicing is extremely important. It all boils down to this: When we are lying on our deathbed, drinking our last drop of water, surrounded by those close to us, and drawing our last, shallow breath, we need to go from light to light and happiness to happiness with the yidams and dakinis coming to welcome us. From now on, we each have to brush the snowflakes off our own coat sleeves. This is important. Please remember this.

May beings take up and practice the stream of nectar
that the sugatas spoke well,
The ore from which comes happiness, dispelling the
torments of the afflictions,
The supreme jewel on the sapling of enlightenment
planted firmly in the mind.
And thus may they break free from all the places where
there is suffering.

Thus spoke the precious lama.

ITHI

A String of Jewels

A Spiritual Biography of Dusum Khyenpa,
the Precious Protector of Living Beings,
Including His Reincarnations

NAMO RATNA GURU

> You who have a brilliant mind, through the supreme vehicle, you see
> All there is to know in the mirror of your heart free of elaborations.
> You know through the five clairvoyances and have perfected the qualities of the path.
> I bow to you, precious one who brings disciples to maturity.

First, our precious lama took ordination from his lama, a great and supreme spiritual friend. He departed for the central land to hear the teachings and undertook hardships. Through the power of having trained in bodhichitta from beginningless time, he was adorned with a profusion of precious qualities. Though much could be said about all of this, here I will select the main points of all that I have heard and present them in brief.

Dusum Khyenpa first listened to the key instructions in the lineage of explanations from Geshe Chapa and others. Then he listened to the instructions from the transmission of practices by the spiritual friend Sharawa. From the precious Lord of Dharma Gampopa, he received the key instructions that penetrate the main points of advice. There are many stories about how he heard all these teachings, but here I will not speak of them. Instead I will write a little about the pure visions he saw.

In the presence of the spiritual friend, Shawa Lingpa, he first met Lama Gomtsul, whom he saw as White Tara.

Later, when Dusum Khyenpa met him, Gampopa asked, "Did you have a vision of Gomtsul Tsultrim Nyingpo?"

Dusum Khyenpa responded, "I saw him as White Tara."

Gampopa responded, "Your meditation on the creation phase is stable." Then when he was staying at Jasang, Dusum Khyenpa had a vision of the Noble Lady. He also had a vision of Coemergent Chakrasamvara. In the sky around, he heard the sounds of damarus and the Sanskrit vowels and consonants, ĀLI and KĀLI. Then when he was traveling to Ngösang, he said that the clairvoyances such as knowing others' minds became clear, and relics appeared.

Further, Dusum Khyenpa stayed in Mön and was supported by its king. When his food had run out, he went down the mountain to replenish his supplies. As he was sitting at the foot of a large tree, a tiger emerged from the forest, circumambulated him three times, and disappeared. On the way up, he said that two people accompanied him back to the place the tiger had come from. He found there a hearth and a large gourd filled with alcohol, which two young women offered him.

Then he departed for Gongkar. He said that as he was descending through the country of Nyemo near Amo on his right were boulders and on his left was a valley. Near the doorway of one house, there appeared four young women who were weaving. One said, "Master, would you like some food?"

"I would," he replied.

One of them went inside and said, "Come in."

He replied, "Bring it out here."

"Nothing bad will happen," she responded. "Do come inside." Then as soon as he went inside, she offered him a generous half gourd containing a stew of human knuckles. Free of doubt, Dusum Khyenpa consumed it. He saw one woman appear as four and the four merge into one. Then holding it up to the sky, one of them offered him a gourd filled with pure white water resembling whey. Drinking it, he found it most delicious.

He said that he saw Chakrasamvara with four faces and twelve arms, embraced by his consort, on the right thumb of the young woman with agile hands. Then as Dusum Khyenpa went through the door outside, all four young women appeared at the doorway. When asked who they were, Gampopa replied that they were the four dakinis of Chakrasamvara.

As soon as he came into the presence of Lama Dzongpa, the lama asked, "Did four dakinis offer you food today?"

"Yes," he replied, "they did,"

"The dakinis gave you a blessing. As for the knuckle stew they offered you, the householder Ashoka's son Dharmasiddhi passed away, and as they were carrying him to the charnel ground of Tartiti, these bones were taken."

Dusum Khyenpa asked, "Are the dakinis here these days?"

The lama replied, "No, they're not. Many dakinis are gathering at Supati charnel ground and they have gone there. As you were leaving to see the king of Mön, the two young women who offered you a drink were also dakinis."

When Dusum Khyenpa thought, "This place resembles my lama's Jakok Retreat," Lama Dzongpa said, "So this place resembles your lama's Jakok Retreat? Now you should do whatever your lama Gampopa says." They spoke of many other things as well.

When Dusum Khyenpa went to offer his respects to him, Gampopa said, "Drölgom and Khampa Gray Hair, you two stay here for a while." The master and his four disciples spent some time together and had many pleasant conversations. Their wide-ranging talk also covered advice, such as how great meditators should not be conceited about their qualities but keep them hidden.

Gampopa said, "When my lama Milarepa was resting in the samadhi of all-encompassing fire, I could not stand the flames and ran away. When he was resting in the samadhi of all-encompassing water, I saw him on pooling water. In this way, he had the qualities that come from resting in the whole range of all-encompassing samadhis. He also possessed extensive clairvoyances, yet he had not even an atom of conceit."

Dusum Khyenpa invited some monks to his bedroom and told stories of his previous meetings with Lama Dzongpa and of the dakinis offering food; he also spoke of Gampopa's advice on how wrong it is to be conceited about one's qualities and how they should be kept hidden.

Then he went to Sangdum to pay his respects to Master Gomtsul. While there, Dusum Khyenpa related how Lama Dzongpa had described just the way things had happened for him and that Lama Dzongpa also knew what the great masters of the past had taught, recounting many stories about them and their wisdom. He also gave key instructions.

Dusum Khyenpa said, "I saw Gampopa as Hevajra present within a circle of light. I also saw Master Gomtsul once as Jetsun Naljorma and three times as Hevajra, and one time as a mass of light. These are my own pure visions. If they were not, others would have to see them, too.

"Once I saw Master Gomtsul as a form of light. When I asked him what that was, the master replied that he was meditating on the all-encompassing samadhi of water. He could meditate on every one of the all-encompassing sense fields."

As soon as Gampopa had passed away, Dusum Khyenpa went to see Master Gomtsul. Master Pakpa said, "Shall we all go together for the fall teachings?" They went together to Porok Dzongchung, Master Pakpa's monastery. While there, he told the story of Gampopa's passing. Dusum Khyenpa shed tears. Master Gomtsul, Pakpa, and Dusum Khyenpa simultaneously saw the great lama before them and offered many prostrations. A moment passed and then, fading away like a rainbow, Gampopa disappeared.

Once at a later time, Dusum Khyenpa went to see Master Gomtsul and said, "I'll go to Kham."

Master Gomtsul replied, "Since this was Gampopa's instruction, you must go one time to Kham. I'll be dead then." At that Rinpoche cried.

Master Gomtsul said, "Don't cry. I'll tell you something astonishing. When I was first practicing, I did as much as I could. Later, I became more capable. These days, I do as I wish. Nowadays, I can see Bodhgaya in a second and, knowing all things to be illusionlike, I am able to do just as I wish."

When Dusum Khyenpa first went to Drushi Retreat, a young woman wearing ornaments offered him nourishment. When he was residing at Gangkar, a young woman offered him sustenance. Also, a dakini offered him nourishment a few times.

While Dusum Khyenpa was traveling to Eastern Tibet, coming along the northern route, he 'dreamt one night that he found the corpse of a plump woman. From within her open rib cage emerged many damarus, playing without a player as their sound faded into space. The master departed along with them and arrived in Uddiyana. There, a young woman appeared who said to him, "From here onward is the region of the wisdom dakinis, and from here downward is the region of the worldly dakinis."

After he had arrived at Kampo Nenang, he had clear visions beyond number. One time he 'dreamt that he met Gampopa, who said, "You should transfer your consciousness to the pure land of Abhirati."

Once there, Rinpoche emanated into space the mandala of Hevajra and eight deities, then manifested himself as Hevajra with eight deities, and entered into the heart of the Hevajra residing in space.

Gampopa commented, "You're really good at that."

One night, Dusum Khyenpa 'dreamt that as they sat underneath a rock overhang and meditated together, he asked Gampopa, "Have you taken a miraculous birth?"

"No," he replied. "I am traveling in the womb."

"Master," Dusum Khyenpa asked, "do you have a spiritual master?"

"No, I don't."

"Then how is it?"

"Mind's natural state knows no interruption." And Gampopa gave the key instruction:

> Giving up the land of your birth, you'll surely be free of desire and hatred.
> If you have real discipline, you'll surely go to the higher realms.
> If you apply skillful means, you'll surely move along the path.
> Resting within the natural ground without altering, you'll surely realize the actual nature.

It was at the retreat of Pompuk that Dusum Khyenpa saw Gampopa and heard him say this verse.

Then the master told what had happened in the afternoon of the eighth day of the seventh month: "Rainbows arose in the form of a parasol and mandala, and Gampopa appeared in their midst."

"What did Gampopa say?"

"He spoke this verse:

Son, the main point of the view is nonduality.
The main point of meditation is nondistraction.
The main point of conduct is union.
The main point of the result is the three undivided."

On the fifteenth day of the seventh month, while commemorating the anniversary of Gampopa's passing, Dusum Khyenpa said, "Four of Gampopa's students will create immense benefit for living beings." He found this amusing and laughed.

Right away, Geshe Sherap Bum asked, "Lama, why is it so funny?"

"I just found it amusing," replied Dusum Khyenpa. "Serkong Yeshe Nyingpo and Yasi Ngönmo will create immense benefit for living beings in the west. Both Gompa Shidze and Dakpo Pakgom will create an immense benefit for living beings in the east. Mönlam Lama, when you have passed away from here, you will be born to the west in Padmini. Having taken birth there, you will become ordained. At this time, your abbot will be Ngaripa Sangpo."

Mönlam Lama asked, "What is my relationship with him?"

Dusum Khyenpa replied, "Four lives prior to this one, he acted as your abbot in Padmini. These days, Ngaripa Sangpo has attained the level of a vidyadhara with power over his lifespan. Mönlam Lama, from the past up to now, you've been a monk for five lifetimes in a row."

One of Gampopa's students, a novice monk, was also the earliest of Dusum Khyenpa's close disciples. Rinpoche said, "These days in the southern world realm, he is engaged in the practice of bodhichitta in the presence of King Surabhibhadra."

Rinpoche said that while he was staying at Pompuk, three mountains appeared. In between the thickening clouds or mist, the sound of the mountain Palgyi Ri resonated in the south. There were a variety of wild beasts, birds, and trees. At its peak was a naked yogini experiencing bliss, with her hair free. Without ornaments, she held a skull cup and raised a curved knife high. Her right leg rested in the crook of her left elbow.

Once he saw Hevajra and his gathering of deities. At Drushi he had a vision of Vajra Yogini. He also saw the Coemergent Chakrasamvara, embraced by his consort. Here on the fifteenth of the seventh month at night, he had a vision of Hevajra embraced by his consort. When a little devotion arose, it faded into a ball of light. He also saw White Tara while staying there.

After the memorial service of the seventh month, he met Master Gomtsul to the north of Bodhgaya in the Grove of the Roaming Buffalo. The Master said, "Your ability to come here is amazing."

After the memorial services during the seventh month in the Dog Year, he saw Jetsun Vajra Yogini with one thousand heads and one thousand eyes as the main figure and surrounded by thirty-six heroines. She spoke to him:

In the tantra of the Heruka,
The mind is said to be free of stains.
A pure emanation of Dharma
Has arisen in the form of Varahi.

This is what he heard. At another time, he saw in space many gatherings of deities. These words resonated:

View and meditation are like sky and water.
Conduct cannot be stopped or established.
The natural state is these three indivisible.
Like the sounds of lutes on a relative level,
What they are and reality itself are inseparable.

This is what he heard.

Once, the sounds of ĀLI and KĀLI resonated in space. Afterward, he had a clear vision of Nairatmya and fifteen deities. She said to him, "As the sounds of the Sanskrit alphabet ĀLI and KĀLI came from my mouth, you were also saying them."

Once, he had the thought, "I should take a look at Tongkun." When he had gone as far as Tsakhar, he wondered if

Geshe Lama would recognize him. And he did, as he showed by smiling and being happy. He had taken birth as the son of a rich man.

When Dusum Khyenpa was residing at Kampo Nenang, he saw Nairatmya in union with the fierce king Achala. While staying at Pompuk, he saw the main figure of the nine-deity mandala of Amrita Kundali in union with Nairatmya. From the mouths of the goddesses resonated the sounds of the Sanskrit vowels and consonants. At first, everything appeared as rainbows and then later faded, just as rainbows do.

During the evening of a feast offering, he saw the mandala of the five deities of Mahamaya.

When Dusum Khyenpa went to Sri Lanka, a yogi came into view. As he wondered who this might be, the yogi appeared as Master Drilbupa. At the same time appeared an ascetic wearing white clothes, who said that he was going to hear Dharma from the Buddha. Rinpoche thought, "Dipamkara has passed away and so has the Buddha." So he asked, "Are you going to see Maitreya?"

"It's possible."

"Are you an emanation of Maitreya?"

"It's possible," he replied.

A ray of sunlight appeared and they departed on its shimmering beam. When they arrived in the presence of the buddha, he turned out to be Maitreya. In a sambhogakaya form with ornaments, Maitreya was teaching the Dharma to numerous monks, and in particular, a verse from his *Supreme Continuum*:

In this, there's nothing to remove
Nor anything at all to add.
Looking authentically at the authentic
And seeing authentically is liberation.

He gave many such teachings with profound meaning. He asked, "Friends, how do you understand this?"

"We understand it to speak of the unborn."

"This is how I understand it, too," Maitreya said.

On a rocky mountain toward the far side of Nepal lived the glorious Great Black Lady at the head of sixty-four mamos. Dusum Khyenpa said that Padmasambhava went there sometimes as he suspected they might be harming living beings.

At the time Rinpoche was staying at Sharwa, he said, "The younger brother of the patron Changma Namkha Bar has taken birth in the Realm of the Thirty-Three Gods. He has excellent shamatha practice and a great deal of wealth."

When Dusum Khyenpa was staying at Pompuk, he said that many came from India to invite him there. Richly ornamented women wearing a great variety of jewels rode in chariots covered with Indian brocades. Umbrellas with swags of pearls accompanied them, and diverse kinds of music could also be heard.

Once in a dream, Dusum Khyenpa sat on a stack of one hundred and eight boulders. At the base of the mountain were eight young women clad in bone ornaments. One after another they offered garlands of flowers to the lama. He tossed the blossoms upward, and they filled all space from the earth to the sky. Then the master flew down from the rocks, and when he had arrived near their middle, he turned around and, facing upward, emanated into the sky a horse from which hundreds more appeared. He departed riding one of them. Later he departed riding a lion. He said that since it was a dream, he could do anything he wished.

Dusum Khyenpa wanted to see the city of Dripten, so he emanated a single body and from that came two, from two came four, and from one hundred came one thousand. He flew just like a swan into the sky and descended on the roof of a house in the middle of the city of Dripten. As soon as he arrived there, he heard the sound of the unborn coming clearly and distinctly from below. Then he flew back into the sky, and on the far side of the city a rocky mountain appeared. There he saw many sights, such as oxen, water buffalo, and numerous other living beings.

Once, on top of a lotus, the stem of which did not touch the bottom of the lake, the master himself was present as Hevajra and his consort. In the sounds of the lutes played by eight goddesses came the words, "To the west is great bliss." Having spoken, the goddesses disappeared into the west. The death that this foreshadowed was averted, and no harm occurred.

When Rinpoche was going to Drung to consecrate a shrine hall, Paldenma and her hundred thousand mamos led him. Everyone there saw the flowers naturally offering themselves.

One evening, it was first clear as far as Daklha Gampo, then it was clear as far as Nepal, and then in all four directions as well as above and below; he had a vision of immeasurable worlds in all six directions. He also saw many lamas who were accomplished masters.

On another evening, he met Gampopa and asked him, "This year is a special one. Why is it that I have met the lama so many times?"

Gampopa replied, "Each time you generate devotion, you will meet the lama."

Rinpoche said, "Dorje Sherap, Öser Lama, and Darma Senge are my disciples for the second time. The yogini Doji Gita was born as the son of the king of Minyak. This allowed her to liberate all the prisoners on the far side of Chunakmo. Her intention was to help the king. Also, she saw that the prisoners would become disciples in a future life."

Dusum Khyenpa said, "I saw a bodhisattva in the form of an ordinary person helping people."

Those present asked, "Please tell us about him."

"These days, the practitioner from Gyal, Dre Chungwa, has three emanations, who are helping living beings. The actual one is from Gyal, the emanation is in China, and the second emanation is in a place between India and Nepal. Previously he took birth as Palpak Tsangpa."

"Why does he have great devotion to you?"

"Previously, from time beyond time, he has been my disciple."

"Also in Tsang, I see that there is one who has attained a bodhisattva level and has two emanations that are benefiting living beings. One of them is directly benefiting people and other living beings in Tsang, and another is doing so at the border of Tibet and Nepal."

As Dusum Khyenpa was leaving for Nepal, the eight goddesses of Hevajra said, "It is not yet time for you to go."

When he opened his eyes, the eight goddesses said, "It is not yet a good time to depart." When he looked to the right, he was surrounded by the goddesses; when he looked to the left, he was surrounded by the goddesses as well.

He also saw Kagyu lamas often. In particular, every time he felt devotion for Gampopa, he saw him.

"In a place twelve days' journey from Uddiyana, Gampopa along with twelve attendants converted a non-Buddhist king through nonconceptual means. Among his disciples Shidze, Genyen Gomra, Gartön, Serkong Yeshe Nyingpo, Simshi Yeshe Nyingpo, Yasi Ngönmo, Gyache, Gyachung, Drakdze, Nyakde Tönpa, Rekgom, and Yönten Nyingpo, six were able to engage in the conduct known as the yogic discipline of awareness in the presence of the lama.

"Gampopa has taken rebirth in Padmini in the west of India and is benefiting living beings. Engaging in conduct like that of Virupa, sometimes he appears as a bhikshu and other times as a yogi. Gampopa engages in a variety of conduct, and his name is Shantivarman. His emanation is benefiting living beings in the pure realm of Placed in Bliss in the west.

He bears the name of Bodhisattva Drime Drakpa. A further emanation is benefiting living beings in a realm of the world to the east known as Ornamented with Ten Million Jewels. He has brought the king Drakpa Taye, his retinue, and all his subjects onto the path. The name of this lama is Bodhisattva Drime Dawey Gyenpa. After his body fades away from there, he will receive the name Buddha Ashokala in the realm of the World of Infinite Thousands.

"Further, in order to convert a non-Buddhist king, Master Gomtsul has taken birth in Kongka, one of the twenty-four places of the dakinis. My lama Penpuk has taken birth right in Tötsang with the name of Gaway Yeshe. Lama Palchenpo has taken birth with the name Palgyi Jungne Bepa in a realm of the world to the north called Ornamented by a Net of Pearls, where he is benefiting many living beings. My lama Trarawa Chenpo was born on the mountain Supri on the border of Chokro Dring in the very western end of this Rose Apple Continent. Named Bodhisattva Drakpa Taye, he has taken birth in the city called Deden and is the guide for some ten million living beings. On the far side of the Kashmiri city of Dripten, Geshe Patsap Lotsawa has taken birth as a pandita named Rinchen Jungne Drakpa. He is helping several living beings.

"Further, my lama Dzongpa has taken birth near the border between Kashmir and Nuche. With his previous consort he is engaged a variety of conduct. He has maintained an immense range of clairvoyances from his previous life. Master Chapa has been reborn in the Kashmiri city of

Dripten as a pandita and is benefiting several living beings. My lama Ngulchuwa took rebirth as the son of the king of Tongkun, fulfilling the king's supplications. In a dream we met at the Five-Peaked Mountain. Geshe Shudön Moripa stays near Potala Mountain in the very western end of this Rose Apple Continent and teaches Dharma through signs. He is benefiting many living beings. My master Sherap Jangchup has been born in the lower part of Bird Foot Mountain and took ordination at the age of eight. He is engaged in practice.

"My lama Rechungpa took rebirth at a place two days' journey on the far side of Nepal and has the name of Ratnasukha. My master Sherap Dorje was born in Penyul. He has a Kadampa teacher and is engaged in practice. My master Pakpa was reborn on the far side of Pamting in Nepal. He is a yogi with a consort and begs alms. My abbot Sapukpa took rebirth as a pandita in the east of India."

One evening, Dusum Khyenpa saw Gampopa and Milarepa. At that time, many different events from different eras all occurred together. When asked about it, he said, "The Great Brahmin Saraha and others from the past gathered last year for a feast offering with yogis from a later time. Then many treatises also appeared, including the Dharmas of Maitreya."

The preceding text has explained just a bit of Dusum Khyenpa's knowledge of the present, and now there follows an explanation of his knowledge of the past: When he was asked where he was born in a previous incarnation, he replied, "Between the continents of Supreme Body to the east and Rose Apple to the south, I was born on a nameless island in a city called Rajaphala, also known as the City of the Excellent King. I lived to the age of one hundred seventy-four. I was just able to engage in yogic conduct.[33] There as well I met Gampopa, and at that time received from him three sadhanas: Mahamaya, Tara the Wish-Fulfilling Wheel, and Vajrasattva. Some of you were also there." They asked which ones, and he replied, "I explained Tara the Wish-Fulfilling Wheel to ten of you: Yönten Ö, Gendun Ö, Yeshe Lama, Mönlam Lama, Jungne Lama, Gyaltsen Lama, Tönpa Tsulseng from Tsang, Geshe Könchok Pal from Tre, Dorje Sherap, and there was a Kadampa there, too.

"About twenty of you were there when I requested Gampopa to perform a feast offering." They asked which ones and he replied, "Geshe Kadampa, Master Rinchen Gyaltsen, Tönpa Sangye, two attendants, Gendun Drak, Mönlam Lama, Dorje Sherap, Geshe Könchok Pal, and Tönpa Tsulseng, who these days is in Ütsang. Two nuns also took part. One is here and another has taken birth in Ü. The patron Gönpawa acted as the sponsor. In making his connections with the lamas, they did what he had requested. As the son of a wealthy householder, he has served as the sponsor here and will also do so in the future. Khenpo Karakpa twice served as my abbot."

When Rinpoche was asked to give his father's name, he said, "My father was Ratna Gupta and my mother was Sumata. My name was Sumatikirti, and we belonged to the merchant caste."

When he was asked, "What is your relationship to Khenpo Sanakpa?"

Rinpoche replied, "To Khenpo Sanakpa, Geshe Yulbarwa, and a third person, I gave refuge and the practice of engaged bodhichitta. One of them did not keep the precepts and these days lives where he did before. The great abbot was a pandita in a former life. I explained to him the bodhisattva levels and The Twenty Stanzas on the Vows.

"Geshe Lama Ö has taken an excellent birth within Domey Setsang near India. He took this rebirth because he was a master there during a previous incarnation. He could be called an accomplished master.

"In the life before that," Dusum Khyenpa continued, "I was born in eastern Supreme Body into the royal caste and took a woman's form. If I had been born a boy, I would have had to take the position of a king. My father's name was Gewachen, my mother's was Sherap Chenma, and mine was Sherap Sangmo. When I was young, my parents died and I met Gampopa, who was a bhikshu called Mana Shree. I took lay vows with him and kept the precepts properly. I had a great number of possessions and exhausted them all in offerings to Gampopa. At that time, many of you and many of my friends were there.

"Once when I was accumulating merit by making an offering to Gampopa, seven of you were there. Three, Gendun Ö, Sherap Lama, and Mönlam Lama, acted as my assistants. Also present were Yönten Ö, Yeshe Ö, Yeshe Öser, and one more, making seven, all of whom were brothers. Your father's name was Kusala Kirti and your mother's, Kusala Bhadri."

In the birth before that one, the master was born on the northwest border of the Rose Apple Continent by the river Adorned with Lotus Flowers. His abbot was the Brahmin Sajjana. At that time, he supplicated Master Dombipa, who was staying under a rock overhang in the mountains.

"Geshe Tsöndru Sherap, Rinchen Gyaltsen, Dok Khepa, and Menge Josey were my students. Geshe Chapa was a minor pandita who was our master. Geshe Dorje Senge was a student of Chapa and has again taken birth near him."

Before that, Dusum Khyenpa took birth as an elephant on the continent of the Bountiful Cow to the west. The patron Gönpa had taken birth as a despotic king who was harming his kingdom. When the king went out with some seven hundred elephants and troops, this elephant was at the head of the troops and trampled the king to death.

Previous to that birth, he was incarnated on the continent of the Bountiful Cow to the west as Dharma Ati and took ordination. He said, "At that time, my master was Telopa and I benefited a few living beings."

And before that birth, Dusum Khyenpa was born in Uddiyana in western India. "I was a yogi and at that time my lama was again Master Telopa. There are four students to whom I gave empowerments then who are here now:

Dorje Bum, Gomngön, Shakya Sherap, and Gompa Chöpal. My name was Shiladanti, and my powers became supreme."

In the birth previous to that, Dusum Khyenpa incarnated into the kingdom of Kalingka as the king Daway Nampar Nönpa. The king's master was Sangye Yeshe Shap, whose master was Jampal Shenyen Avadhutipa.

When this king went to circumambulate the triumphant and glorious Drepung Stupa, from the sky resonated these words: "You have not yet attained siddhis. Go and gather the conditioned roots of goodness." And so he established a monastery for many monks and gathered great virtue and the roots of goodness. Then, returning to the stupa, he circumambulated it many times and received all the ordinary siddhis without exception. Two dogs who had left along with him attained ordinary siddhis. These days, they have been reborn in Uddiyana as two worldly dakinis who are rougher than the others.

"Many who were in the king's retinue then are here now. Many were also from Kartiwa and numerous others were from the lower lands and elsewhere. At that time, Tönpa Sangye and Geshe Rinchen Gyaltsen both had many ordinary siddhis."

"Why don't they have them now?" he was asked.

"The siddhis came from the practice they did at that time.

"Then, Gampopa was Master Sangye Yeshe Shap and Jampal Shenyen Avadhutipa was Lama Yila. You thirteen made supplications, which were fulfilled, not all at once but some earlier and some later.

"Among Tönpa Sangye, Rinchen Gyaltsen, Yönten Ö, Yönten Lama, Gendun Drak, and Mönlam Lama, these days, one is in Ü. I'm one from Treho. I had been born as Daway Nampar Nönpa, the king of the country of Kalingka, and have taken seven more births since then."

Dusum Khyenpa was asked, "Precious master, after this life, where will you take birth?"

"I'll be born in the northeast of Uddiyana to the west of India in a city called Kartika. Gampopa will have already taken birth in the city of Padmini and have the name of Shantivarman. In this city, Gampopa will have discussions with a non-Buddhist pandita. Gampopa will be the one defending a thesis and the non-Buddhist pandita will be the one attacking it. The debate will begin and Gampopa will come out the winner, so the non-Buddhist teacher will become Buddhist and receive the name Dharmaraja. The name of the non-Buddhist king will be Mahajina.

"In the city of Kartika, there will live a pandita called Bodhivajra who will have many qualities within.

"In the city of Padmini, Gampopa will convert the non-Buddhist king and at the same time the pandita will convert the king of the country of Kartika. Gampopa Rinpoche, the Buddhist pandita, and a non-Buddhist pandita will all be supported by the king.

"Between the cities of Padmini and Kartika there is a country of few cities, which is inhabited by non-Budddhists who will later convert. It will take about two days to travel between the two cities, which are on the northwest border of Uddiyana.

"The name of the master's father will be Dharmasiddhi, his mother's, Mahaprajna, and he will be called Prajnashila. At that time, I will meet Gampopa," he said. "The patron Gönpa will take birth as the son of a minister and became ordained as a monk. Some of you will also take birth here in the city of Karnapa. These three cities are found together in one area."

A monk asked, "After this, what rebirths will we take?" "You and Yönten Ö, Gendun Ö, Mönlam Lama, Yeshe Ö, Tönpa Tsulseng, and Gendun Drak will all be born simultaneously in the merchant caste and take a great number of births here in this area. Master Rinchen Gyaltsen, Tönpa Sangye, Tönpa Jangchup Drak, Tönpa Sönam, Pön Dharmaraja, Shakya Sherap, Gomngön, Dorje Bum, Geshe Rinchen Drak, Wangchuk Drak, Öser Lama, Yönten Lama, Darma Senge, Dorje Tsöndru, Jangpa Lhaso, and many others have been reborn. For those of you who are to meet Gampopa many times, if you haven't done so yet, you will in the future."

"Precious master, where will you take your next birth?"

"In the middle of Tibet, I will be born in Lhodrak in seven places of practice. I won't stay long and will meet some of you there."

"After that, where will you be born?"

"I will take birth in a realm of this world to the east, where patron Gönpa will take birth as a king, and I will keep him on an authentic path. I'll meet you there again. Then many lives will occur when you do not need me and I will also be helping many others."

The precious lama's life is like an island of jewels.
The Shakya monk Gendun Ö
And the Shakya monk Mönlam Lama
Told me what they had heard from the precious lama.
I, Dechungwa, collected their words and wrote them down.

Through this virtue imbued with devotion, a stainless moon,
Having seen his face and heard his words,
May the lord's disciples be in harmony and find faith.
May they enter the path of the mahayana, this great tree,
And lead a life that is just like his.

This concludes The Middle-Length String of Jewels: A Spiritual Biography of Dusum Khyenpa, the Precious Protector of Living Beings, Including His Reincarnations.

A Collection of Songs

I prostrate to the lord gurus.
Please guide the fortunate along the path.

From the Akanishta Dharma palace,
He holds the entire treasury of secret mantra.
His activity is continuous:
I bow to the bhagavan Vajradhara.

From the eastern city of Sahor,
He realized the inseparability of the three kayas
In the monastery of Shri Nagaracha.
The heart son of Vajradhara
Sends forth a billion emanations:
I bow to the lord Telopa.

Through the power of reciting the creation phase
In the retreat of Pullahari,
The dakini made the prophecy.
He looked for Telo in the east.

He actually met the nirmanakaya Telo,
Who is like the crown jewel of qualities.

He relied on the lama up through twelve,
Taking in the experience of the twelve trials.

Through receiving the guru's blessings,
He experienced the spontaneously present great bliss.
He perfected every yogic discipline:
I bow at glorious Naro's feet.

Born on the border of Mön and Do,
He searched for Dharma in India
Without regard for life or limb
And met the gurus who were siddhas.

By mastering the four classes of tantra,
He received glorious Naro's blessings
And realized all phenomena are illusory:
I bow at the feet of Lord Marpa.

Born on the border of Mang and Gung,
He searched for true Dharma in Nepal and Tibet.
He touched the feet of Lord Marpa
In front of the retreat place in Lhodrak.

He listened to the profound Dharma, the three cycles of mother tantras,
Requested instructions on the six yogas of Naro,
And went to the border of Nepal and Tibet.
In the hermitage at the peak of the red cliffs
He did the practices of the winds.

Blessed by the dakas and dakinis,
He gained the supreme and ordinary siddhis.

He emanated various forms
And guided the fortunate on the path:
I bow at the feet of Milarepa.

Rejecting royal power as filth,
He studied only the five sciences,
Practiced Chakrasamvara,
And achieved the dharmakaya of yogic conduct.

When Lady Tara made a prophecy
And Jangchup Ö made the request,
He acted out of bodhichitta,
Disregarding his own self,
And went to Tibet to swiftly benefit others.

He raised the torch of wisdom and
Dispelled the gloom of ignorance.
He is the heart son of Serlingpa:
I bow at the feet of glorious Atisha.

The three translators Khu, Ngok, and Drom,
The lineages of the upper and lower monasteries,
And all the masters up to the three brothers
Made the teachings spread and flourish:
I prostrate to the spiritual friends of the past.

Born in Sho, at glorious Radreng Monastery,
He touched the feet of the three brothers
Who followed Dipamkara.
The heart son of both Chen and Nga,
He realized the union of the two truths

And helped others through the four means of nurturing:
I bow to Nyukrumpa, the spiritual friend.[34]

Born in the center of Nyal,
He studied the conventional there.
In search of instructions, he went to Ürutö
And touched the feet of many masters.

He taught the concise meaning of the three baskets
And studied with both middling and greater individuals.
To ripen beings with compassion,
He earnestly engaged in the three trainings.

Since that alone did not cut conceptual elaborations,
He went to the border of Drin and Nye
And touched the feet of Lord Milarepa,
Who blessed him with a prophecy.

He studied channels and winds and phowa,
Went all the way through the paths and levels,
And achieved the three kayas.[35]

I prostrate to the guru buddhas
Who ripen beings with compassion.

Spoken by Dusum Khyenpa.

OM SVASTI

I prostrate with sincere devotion
To the medicine that cleanses body, speech, and mind,
The supreme lamp that illuminates
The darkness of the three realms of samsara.

After the passing of innumerable buddhas,
Those who have become entirely clear
Delight in Dharma wherever they are born
And protect from poverty all they befriend.
Their compassion wells up spontaneously,
And they accomplish only what helps others.
They are beautified by seven jewels.
Due to their mandala of love and compassion,
Friend and foe alike turn their minds to them.
They've entirely given up self-love and flattery
And take joy in Dharma without hypocrisy.
Such are the characteristics of the mahayana family.

There's nothing to turn to in this transient life—
A rainbow shining clear in the sky
Vanishes in a single instant.
A river's current and dewdrops
Will disappear in but a moment.

The dream you dreamt one hour last night
Is just a memory when you wake.
Your confused perceptions of the six types of beings
Are ego-clinging that has not been destroyed.
But if you cut its root, confusion too
Has emptiness and compassion as its core.

If you meditate, there is no doubt
You will achieve your own and others' benefit.

The phenomena of samsara and nirvana
And the yoga of your own mind are confusion:
If you understand mind to be like space, confusion
  is stilled.
Freedom from the two extremes is the middle way.
The mind appearing as samsara and nirvana is
  mind only.
Eliminating exaggeration is validity.[36]

Since it is unidentifiable bliss, it is mother tantra.
Since it is clear with no fixation, it is father tantra.
Since all views are perfected within it,
It is the instruction of the Kama great perfection.[37]

If such realization arises,
The suffering of the three realms of samsara is pacified,
So it is also called "pacification."

All samsara and nirvana
And all the perceived and perceivers
Are the supreme lack of elaboration transcending
  mind—
The indivisibility of emptiness and compassion.
If you realize that, it is the three *dohas*.[38]

Any of the different paths of means
Are instructions to produce this.

The three baskets and four tantras of the Buddha's words
Are explanations that bring understanding of this.

Whether it is instructions or explanations,
Have devotion for the lamas,
Care for the six classes of beings with compassion,
And meditate vividly on the creation phase.
Treasure resting in the mind's nature.

You said please send instructions,
And though it is not appropriate to write
These instructions of the three vajra words,
You are a faithful and intelligent person
Fully in harmony with the Dharma. Thus I ask
The lord guru and the dakinis to forgive me.

Sent by the Rinpoche from Kham to the patron Sherap Khar.

ITHI

OM SVASTI
May there be the auspiciousness of the lamas
Who by coming as nirmanakaya gurus
Free all beings and individuals with karma
From the demon of clinging to reality.

May there be the auspiciousness of the lady
Whose nature is wisdom.
Through her natural love, she brings beings
To liberation in appropriate ways.

May there be the auspiciousness of the goddess
Who fulfills wishes as she sits
Gracefully with her legs half crossed
On the lotus and moon seat of means and wisdom.

May there be the auspiciousness of Tara,
The supreme mother with a blue-green hue and
  majestic face.
She is beautiful with gems, jewelry, and necklaces.
Her right hand protects from fear, her left hand
  holds an utpala.[39]

May there be the auspiciousness of the yidam deities,
As those who meditate on them with respect
Will accomplish the four activities
That are declared in the secret mantra.

May there be the auspiciousness in the future
Of meeting them, becoming one in essence,

And then becoming indistinguishable from them
In the four activities of guiding beings.

May there be the auspiciousness of the Dharma
protectors
Who were commanded by the Sugata
And in the presence of the Master of the Secret[40]
Promised to guard the teachings.

May the auspiciousness of never parting for an instant
From the lamas, yidams, and Dharma protectors
And of blocking ordinary thoughts
Bring joy and goodness.

Written by the precious Dusum Khyenpa.

The precious lama said that he sang this song while spending three summers and winters in a sealed retreat at Jasang in Penyul.

These thoughts occurred to this beggar:

Knowing that samsara has no nature,
I'm freed of the wish to build up the eight concerns.

Nirvana is not somewhere else—
I'm freed of the wish for effort and exertion.

I've found the Buddha in my own mind—
I'm freed of the wish to achieve siddhi.

Thoughts have the nature of dharmakaya—
I'm freed of the wish to distinguish good and bad.

I've realized existence and peace are the same, not two—
I'm freed of the wish to distinguish levels and phases.

I had an experience of the four mudras—
I'm freed of the wish to prove or refute.

I've realized the two truths are inseparably the same—
I'm freed of the wish to traverse the five paths.

I've grasped the mind essence, the natural state—
I'm freed of the wish to take a foothold.

I've realized that knowing one frees all—
I'm freed of the wish to study.

Knowing this form as an illusory body,
I'm freed of the wish to cherish it.

I've understood sound to be empty resonance;
I've understood friends and respect as confusion;

The dharma nature, let alone, has become clear—
I'm freed of the wish to divide sessions from breaks.

My mind is like that, child—
You must understand this, too.

After the precious guru, the physician Gampopa, said, "You go meditate on the border of Mön and Tibet," Dusum Khyenpa received offerings from the king of Mön and went to stay on a mountain in Mön. While he was there, a friend asked him to sing a song, and he sang this:

I prostrate to the lords, the lamas.
I take refuge in those whose kindness we need.

The mountain over there is Mön;
The mountain over here, Tibet.
In the inexhaustible realm
On the border of Tibet and Mön,
The yogi free of reference roams,
Keeping himself to mountain retreats
Where there is no one else to please.

I've never sung a tune before,
But on request from Tsultrim Sal
This melody has now come to mind.

"The mountain over there is Mön,"
A place I've never been before—
It means the extreme of nirvana.

"The mountain over here, Tibet,"
The source of various thoughts and ideas—
It means the extreme of samsaric realms.

"In the inexhaustible realm
On the border of Tibet and Mön"
Means in the pure realms of the buddhas.

"The yogi free of reference roams,
Keeping himself to mountain retreats
Where there is no one else to please"
Means overpowering the eight concerns.

If you can't keep to a mountain retreat,
You won't gather the sky by collecting it.
You won't catch the wind by grasping it.
You won't see the mind's nature by looking at it.
Blocking won't stop the six consciousnesses.

If you meditate, then let mind be.
If it gets scattered, then let mind go.

Viewing samsara and nirvana
Without any clinging is happiness.
To meditate never separate from
Nonthought is happiness.
Effortless and spontaneous
Conduct is happiness.
As pure of clinging as the sky,
The result is happiness.

If you can realize something like that,
The manifold music is amazing.
The fear of death has been removed;
Samsara becomes self-liberated.

Accept this gift of song, Lord Guru;
I offer it to the learned and great.
Please take delight, you on your thrones.

Then Dusum Khyenpa returned to his lama, who said, "You go to Shamey Snow Mountain to meditate," so he went there. He spent the three summer months there and then went out to look for provisions. When he got just below his retreat, he thought, "What is this? I have the special instructions. I know how to extract the inexhaustible elixir. I have met a lama who is like a buddha, and special experience and realization have been born in me." Then he sang this song.

Precious lama with a lineage,
Source of all the fortunate need or want,
Your blessings come without any bias—
If I have little faith or devotion, it's my own fault.

You teach the winds and channels, the king of instructions
From the king of secret mantra, the mother tantra.
When bliss and heat blaze in the body,
If I have little perseverance, it's my own fault.

I'm ungrateful to my father; my body, speech, and mind are weak.
I may not have three layers of wool,
But I have the instructions on spontaneous chandali—
If I am afraid of freezing, it's my own fault.

Though I have no wealth of my own to spend
And have no support from the faithful,
I know how to extract inexhaustible elixir—
If I am afraid of hunger, it's my own fault.

My sufferings in samsara have been unbearable,
But now that I have met Rinpoche,
If I do not have enough fortitude
To practice wholeheartedly, it's my own fault.

Though my realization may not be stable,
I have the instructions on the three bardos.
Since I have practiced as my lama said,
If I am afraid of death, it's my own fault.

Lama Rinpoche sang this "Song of Five Happinesses" while staying at the Tsurphu Ngösang retreat.

Awareness soars in the empty expanse—
There's no mention of the cause, the five poisons.
Confidence in the view is happiness.

Great bliss soars in the nondual expanse—
There's no mention of places to go astray.
Confidence in meditation is happiness.

The spontaneous soars in the unborn expanse—
There's no mention of proof or refutation.
Confidence in conduct is happiness.

The dharmakaya soars in the wisdom expanse—
There's no mention of this life or the next.
Confidence in the result is happiness.

The yogi soars in the expanse of the realm—
There's no mention of friends or relatives.
Cutting ties to your homeland is happiness.

It is said that Rinpoche spoke this while making offerings in Nenang during the time of the constellation Anuradha.

Yesterday on the Anuradha full moon,
I made offerings to the Three Jewels
To fulfill the guru's intentions.
In the evening I prayed to the guru;
At dawn in a dream as I slept,
I saw the guru come to me
And speak these words:

"Know view as awareness free of extremes.
Know meditation as the natural state free of change.
Know conduct as the four streams free of desire.
Know fruition as the three inseparable.
Know this as the dharmakaya, the benefit for oneself.

"Perform activity to benefit others:
Free of attachment, give generously.
Free of harming, maintain discipline.
Free of anger, cultivate patience.
Free of indolence, be diligent.
Free of distraction, meditate with concentration.
Free of elaboration, give rise to the wisdom of great bliss.
Dedicate these six for the benefit of others."

It is said that he heard Gampopa say this.[41]

Lama Rinpoche said this while staying in Nenang:

NAMO GURU

Samsara and nirvana are inseparable.
Perhaps I'm free of both hope and fear.

The yidam is a mental perception.
Perhaps I should drop the creation stage.

Obstacles are siddhi.
Perhaps I should drop the protection circle.

The winds and the mind are inseparable.
Perhaps I should drop meditation on channels
and winds.

Faults themselves are qualities.
Perhaps I have blocked the sidetrack of experience.

Appearance and mind are mixed inside.
Perhaps I'm free of perceiver and perceived.

Self and other are not two.
Perhaps I'm free of desire and hatred.

I'm on the threshold of no further lives.
Perhaps in one life I've finished the paths and levels.

It's primordially spontaneously present.
Perhaps it is free of causes and conditions.

I'm in the middle between something and nothing.

Perhaps this is what transcends mind.
Equipoise and postmeditation blend together.
Perhaps I have achieved stability of mind.

Conduct is the six consciousnesses relaxing.
Perhaps attributes have been naturally liberated.

I am free of virtue and misdeeds.[42]
The four conducts have become natural.
Perhaps I am free of pompousness.

The five objects belong to the state of illusion.
Perhaps fixation on the transient has stopped.

Luminosity is continuous.
Perhaps the three bardos do not exist.

I have resolved everything to be my mind.
Perhaps I know one and am learned in all.

I don't need to think about eloquence.
Perhaps a cook has got into the Dharma.

When Rinpoche was residing at Tsola Karpo, he sang:

Ema! In the charnel ground of aggregates
Is the nature of the mind, the self-arisen king.
It used to be swayed by the breeze of thought
But now has the meaning of great bliss.

Awareness, the precious minister,
Used to be scattered in the expanse of memory
But now is aware of everything, self and other.

The retinue of eight consciousnesses
Used to disperse to their own domains,
But now they gather in the plain, never leaving.

The queen of the all-ground, the empty consort,
Used to be tainted by the inappropriate
But now has regained her home, the mind's nature.

The unbridled mind of the horse
Used to race down the wrong path
But now has been caught by the true bridle.

The precious jewel of the mind's nature
Used to be lost in the crowd of afflictions
But now has been grasped on its own ground.

Looking at the ground is an experience of delight.
Looking at the meaning is exceedingly amusing.

Jetsun Rinpoche sang this at the request of Geshe Bö while staying at Pompuk.

I've realized the power of self-awareness, free of extremes,
And understand this to be the utmost view.
How could philosophers get this?

I rest continually in the natural state
And understand this to be the utmost meditation.
How could those who vacillate get this?

I've dedicated body and mind to the benefit of beings
And understand this to be the utmost conduct.
How could those who are selfish get this?

I've realized these three are inseparably one
And understand this to be the utmost result.
How could those who hope and fear get this?

Isn't that how it is, meditator named Bö?
If you realize this, it is the utmost.

This was spoken in terms of the four: view, meditation, conduct, and result.

Dusum Khyenpa's Spiritual Biography in Verse

Though the sun's mandala shines ever bright,
From a north-facing cave ever dark, its light isn't seen.
With warmth and moisture, a tree swiftly grows;
Know that the unfortunate are like the cave and the good vessels, like the tree.

The Summary:
On the eastern continent, he was a great bhikshu.
On *the island of* Dhari, he gave rise to bodhichitta with Sura.[43]
In Uddiyana, he was *a yogi* working as the smith Utita
And on the *western* Bountiful Cow, *bhikshu* Dharmashri.
On the western continent, the elephant subdued the king.
At Kalingka, he was King Dawa *Nampar* Nönpa;
Near the river Adorned with Lotus Flowers, he became a bhikshu.
On the eastern continent, he was *the king's* daughter, Sherap Sangmo
And there, too, he was *the bhikshu* Ratnashila

Born to parents in Treshö, *as a son* named Gepel,
He learned to cast spells *through Lhamo* from
Gompo Gepo
And received instructions from Lama Bero *and Paldzin.*
He saw Palden Lhamo clearly manifest.
As thanks for an enemy's death, he raced a horse.
At the place of Kadrak, he took novice monk's vows
from Choklo Sengdrak.
In Trarawa he listened to the genuine Dharma.
He went to Tölung to be with *Puyi* Gyamar *and Chapa*
And received oral instructions from Sharawa *and his
disciple Penyul Sherap Dorje.*
With Geshe Sapukpa he took full ordination
And studied with the glorious Galo and Aseng.

In the presence of Sharwa *Lingpa*, he saw Gomtsul as
White Tara
And met Gampopa and Gomchung *at Gampo.*
Rinpoche received oral instructions from Rechungpa
and Namkha Sal.
He met *Uyuk* Penpukpa and *Gyapmo* Yangkhangpa.
He studied directly *with* both Shen and Relchak.
Dakinis offered him nourishment *while meditating*
at Ölkhar.
He saw Gampopa as Hevajra.
In Mön *dakinis offered food and* a tiger circled
round him.
He turned back lightning at Pakrikha.
At Latö he met *both* the novice monk brothers.

Meditating at Jasang Rock his qualities *of insight*
increased.
Shamey Gangkar offered her respects *at Jomo Gang.*
As he went to Nyemo *Nyidrung,* dakinis made offerings
of food.
He received key instructions from Lama Dzong *at*
Nyemo Dar.

At Dzongchung the three*, master and disciples,* saw
Gampopa *in the sky.*
He saw Varahi with two faces at Drushi;
Here, too, he 'dreamt a serpent swallowed him
without harm.
In Ngösang *at Tsurphu* many relics came forth.
On the northern route, damarus emerged and he went
to Uddiyana.
At Nenang he saw Hevajra and eight deities;
Here, too, he saw Hevajra embraced by his consort.
He saw the *red* Varahi Khechari
And White Tara at Pompuk.
He dreamt he met Gomtsul in Bodhgaya.
He saw Varahi with one thousand arms and eyes
And Gampopa with a retinue of two.
He had a vision of Nairatmya with fourteen goddesses.
He met Master Dorje Drilbupa.
He saw noble Achala and his consort.
In Tushita he heard Maitreya teach.
He saw Amrita Kundali and consort.
Turn by turn, dakinis offered garlands of flowers.
He saw many buddhas and bodhisattvas.

In a rock shelter he met Gampopa *and saw many deities.*
He saw Great Maya along with her retinue *of four.*
He heard the sound of dakinis playing lutes *and averted this sign of death.*
As he consecrated *a statue of Khasarpani,* the flowers offered themselves.
The consecration went very well; *some saw visions.*
He saw Gönpo Driguk Dzin at Nenang,
And *here* Jetsun Mila appeared as well.
While dreaming he saw wondrous things in Kashmiri Dripten.
At Kampo he reversed Rahula's obstacles.
When leaving for Central Tibet, he subjugated Dorje Paltsek *and slipped away.*
He saw glorious and supreme Hayagriva with four deities.

In Central Tibet he resolved the strife in Tsal.
He saw Avalokiteshvara in Lhalung and went
To an Indian *feast* offering in the Year of the Bird.
At Tangchung in Latö, the teacher saw *his emanation.*
He had a clear vision of Pakmo Döndrup.
He saw Tara with eight arms, and
The four classes of dakinis made offerings to him.
He saw Hevajra encircled by eight goddesses
And the Medicine Buddha of beryl blue light.
He met the Great Mother of the Buddhas of the three times.
In Buddha Nahi he met the king *Indrabodhi.*
In Dowo *he had a vision of* four-faced Vajra Varahi.

Three times, a teaching was *spontaneously* sealed
with secrecy.
At the Five-Peaked Mountain he saw Lama Bero
in a dream.
He met *two-armed* Great Tara in person
And *saw* the mandala of Chakrasamvara,
Avalokiteshvara *with eleven heads*, one thousand
arms and eyes
And *Coemergent* Chakrasamvara with consort.

As he was giving empowerments, *many* visions were seen.
He saw the mandala of Guhyasamaja,
Vajra Varahi with one face,
The mandala of *Yamantaka*, the glorious Black-Haired
One,
And the goddess Kurukulle.
At Palri, he met Saraha;
The Lord Maitripa gave him instructions.
In a dream he clearly *saw Daklha* Gampo.
His emanations included a yogi of Lente,
A bhikshu living in Ngari,
A yogi *emanated* in the east of India, and
A king on a continent to the east.
He saw innumerable appearances of Varahi.
In front of Dowo a forest is filled with Taras.
Before *they appeared*, he knew the dakinis as a sign
of death.
At the cremation, a variety of miracles occurred.
His Drepung Stupa has great blessing.

These days he resides at Karti in India.
After, he will come to the places of practice in Lhodrak.
Again in the east there are seven stupas.
After Maitreya, he will be the *Buddha* Lion.
Gomchung was reborn on Bird Foot Mountain.
In the country of Kongkana, Gomtsul took rebirth.
Gampopa was born in the city of Padmini
And has three emanations; it is said that finally
He will be fully awakened in the *World of* Infinite Thousands.
That is the spiritual biography of Dusum Khyenpa.
May it adorn the world and blaze in auspicious glory.

Glorious Dusum Khyenpa's lives, activities, and visions, which are wondrous and immeasurable, are beyond words. In order to nourish the devotion of the fortunate ones, they have been abridged and written down by the Shakya bhikshu Galo at Tsurphu.

Dialogues with Gampopa

I prostrate to the exalted lamas.

When I was in the retreat of blessings,
Wind entered the central place and brought
Nonthought and bliss. I thus saw the nature,
Realized its meaning, and then asked the guru.

I have recorded a few questions and answers that I am afraid of forgetting.

Through my meditation, something occurred that I could not describe: free of all thoughts, naturally luminous, and blissful in essence—all three indivisible. When that happened, there were many bodhisattvas in the sky reciting mantras, making music, and saying "Pir ti ri." When I asked what all that was, my master replied, "It is the wind entering the central channel. You have controlled the breath a bit too much and it has become forced."

"What is the difference between forced breathing and gentle breathing?" I asked.

"Forced breathing is holding both the upper and lower

breath with pain as long as you can," he replied. "It is like, for instance, when a dam is distended by water and then spills over and breaks. Many faults occur, so there is the danger of leprosy or other problems. Gentle breathing is holding one third of the breath above and two thirds below as long as it is comfortable. If it becomes painful, exhale slowly. It will not go wrong, so that is the best." I asked what the focus of the attention is in the two, and he replied that they are similar.

"How many occasions are there when the winds enter the central channel?" I asked.

"There are either four or eight occasions when it happens naturally," he replied. "The four occasions when it enters are when awakening to buddhahood, when getting intoxicated, when fainting, and during sexual intercourse. The eight are, in addition to those, when the winds shift to the left, when strong anger occurs, during deep sleep, and when the eyes see form but do not grasp it. They enter on these eight occasions, but since one does not realize the nature as it is, they are called an approximation of pristine wisdom.

"In this context, the lama's instructions act as the coemergent condition for the winds to enter on three occasions: through the power of vase breathing, through apprehending luminosity and dreams, and through the power of meditating on the winds, and so forth. When they enter on occasions such as these, it is realization of the unaltered meaning as it is," he said.

"What is more powerful," I asked, "controlling the winds by focusing on chandali or controlling the winds by meditating on nonthought?"

"Chandali is more powerful. If you hold the breath with a sharp, undistracted focus on chandali, at first heat arises in a roar, then it produces bliss, and then nonthought automatically comes. Thus chandali is more effective," he replied.

"When you know that heat first arises, how long do you rest in the understanding of bliss and emptiness?" I asked.

"You cannot put a limit on it," he replied. "For example, in springtime, the earth and water warm and melt the ice, allowing sprouts to grow. Then leaves, branches, and flowers grow and the fruit ripens. Similarly, heat arises out of the breath and chandali. Then bliss accompanied by pain arises clearly at the navel. At that point, hold the mind on the bliss in the four chakras and then spread it, so that bliss fills the entire body. Then all thought automatically stops, and this is called undefiled great bliss. It automatically arises from what precedes it, but you cannot point it out as being such and such. This is exactly what is taught as entering the central channel."

"Are the nonthought of controlling the winds and the nonthought of not controlling the winds similar?" I asked.

"They are not. The nonthought of not controlling the winds is a neutral feeling called lethargic nonthought. When you control the winds to eliminate faults such as torpor and agitation, nonthought occurs with its specific characteristics manifest," he said. "Which is better?" I asked. "Blocking the six consciousnesses and entering nonthought internally, or resting freely without fixation, not stopping the six consciousnesses?"

"Resting internally like that is collecting the all-ground into the seed of mindfulness, and then resting in nonthought. That is not right—even the listeners and non-Buddhists have that. It is not letting the six consciousnesses rest freely," he said.

"It is said that we need the results of all our Dharma practice at the time of death. So when a great meditator dies, what is the most effective phowa to perform before the pain of death or before the mind gets disturbed?"

"Do twenty-eight HIK KA and the inconceivable phowa."

"How do you do those two?"

"According to the explanation in the commentary on the *Sambuṭa*, think that there are twenty-seven lotuses with four petals each stacked in your spine. Nearby the center of all the lotuses is your mind, the letter A. Block the lower gates with the hero's armor and the upper gates such as the mouth with the heroine's armor and so forth. Draw a forceful hik breath. Say 'HIK KA' forcefully, and think that the a in the center of the lotuses is drawn up the string into each successive lotus. While training, control it and then say, 'KA HIK.' Draw in the upper breath and the A descends. If you are unable to do phowa because of age, guide it up with twenty-one HIK KAS, but do not make it descend with KA HIK. Do this over and over. When performing phowa, lead it up twenty-eight times and then send the mind to whichever place you wish," he said.

"Does that transfer you there?" I asked.

"That doesn't quite do it," he replied. "Agitating the heart will make it quiver. After that, do the inconceivable phowa. That will eliminate doubt."

"Should a great meditator who meditates on nonthought do that?" I asked.

"My great lama said that if you are apprehensive of the pain of death, you could do phowa prior to it, but he did not like that."

"Well then, what should one do?"

"At the time of death, lie on your side in the posture of the sleeping lion with your right side underneath. Separate the body and mind and send your mind to Tushita or whichever place you want to go. Resting in nonthought there is best."

"Does that make the phowa happen?"

"It is called gathering flowers in winter. When you touch flowers that ripened in the fall, they fall apart because they've gone rotten. Similarly, at the time of death, the points comprised of the elements cause the mind and body to separate, so the pain of death will not occur and you will transfer quickly," he said.

"How should one understand enforced phowa and trained phowa?" I asked.

"Enforced phowa is making the mind of a wicked or ordinary person throw off the body so it falls to the ground like a log. Trained phowa is when a great meditator trains through controlling the HIK KA, the sixth exercise, or through burning," he replied.

"How does the bardo occur when you have done phowa?"

"There are three types of bardos. Now is the bardo of birth and death, which is this bardo itself. It is like a dream, of course. The path is meditating on the instructions of dream bardo now and thereby apprehending luminosity during dreams. The bardo of becoming is mixed with the luminosity of the result."

"Once you have apprehended dreams, how should you meditate later when you are awake?"

"Later when you wake up, meditate thinking, 'What is the difference between last night's dream and these appearances right now?' There's no difference at all."

"Well then, Lord Ngokpa and his disciples said to meditate on sleep as the dharmakaya and dreams as the sambhogakaya. Is that it?" I asked.

"Sleep is ignorance, so how can you meditate on it as the dharmakaya? That's called Dharma that is taught without any meditation experience. Apprehending dreams and then recognizing the dharmakaya luminosity is meditation. At that time, dreams, the illusory body, and the luminosity of the result are mixed, so it is mixing."

"How do the elements dissolve at the time of death? What are the signs of appearance, increase, attainment, and luminosity like?" I asked.

"At the time of death, the earth dissolves into water, so you cannot hold the body up. Water dissolves into fire, so your nose and mouth get dry. At that point, there are the signs of appearance. The external sign is like moonlight, and the internal sign is like fireflies. Of the eighty thoughts, the thirty-three that come from hatred cease. Air dissolves into consciousness, so the body's heat dissipates. The external sign of increasing appearance is like sunlight, and the inner sign is like a lamp. The forty thoughts that come from desire cease. Beings from Khechari come to escort great meditators, and Yama's henchmen come for the wicked.

"The mandala of wind perishes, so the exhalation is long and inhalation short. The external sign of the attainment of appearance is like darkness. The internal sign is like butter lamps. The seven thoughts that come from delusion cease. While you remain there with only the internal breath, the HAṂ at the crown gained from the father collapses. That and the essence of chandali received from the mother at the navel—the two letters of means and wisdom—meet at the heart, due to which the complexion of the corpse stays radiant for one, two, three, four, five, or six days.

"After that, there is the result luminosity. The external sign is like dawn, and the internal sign is like a sky free of clouds. There, the path luminosity and result luminosity mix. That luminosity is naturally luminous, free of all thought, and filled with undefiled bliss. Appearances as well occur with the nature of bliss. Appearances cannot harm you in hell—it is seeing the appearances as suffering that binds you. Appearances do not affect a buddha, because appearances arise as bliss, so they are liberated."

"Are the current path luminosity, the luminosity of the winds entering the central channel, the occasion of the third empowerment, and the luminosity of dreams similar in essence to result luminosity? And how long does the result luminosity last?" I asked.

"The essence is similar. Even now, the path and result are like the occasion when the winds enter the central channel—they last a short time. It's like the moon on the first day of the lunar month. If it mixes with the result luminosity, it lasts a long time. The shortest would be three and a half days. It's said to resemble the full moon.

"At that point, for those who have instructions, clarity is the nirmanakaya, bliss the sambhogakaya, nonthought the dharmakaya, and the indivisibility of the three the essence kaya. All four are present, so that is called the bardo of the perfection of all qualities. Reciting the Names of Manjushri says:

> Complete awakening in an instant;
> The difference is made in an instant.

"A doha says:

> From a single instant of knowing,
> It is as if you permeate the mandala of all that can
> be known;
> You have no thoughts but know everything clearly.

"That's it," he said.

"How do the two form kayas bring benefit to sentient beings?" I asked.

"Although there is no thought of action or acting, they appear adorned with the marks and signs to bodhisattvas on the tenth level with pure perception. They appear in one billion worlds and elsewhere as the six sages.[44] That is how they bring benefit," he replied.

Then I asked, "Which master's assertion is that?"

"Lama Tepupa and Lama Adula Vajra in the lineage of Naropa," he replied. "My position is that the current path luminosity, the bardo luminosity, and the result luminosity mix. Lama Balpo says that right now is the result, and so the two of us spend all day debating this over and over again," he said, telling the story.

"What happens if you do not apprehend the result luminosity?" I asked.

"If you now recognize path luminosity when the winds enter the central channel through the condition of the lama's instructions, it is impossible not to apprehend the result luminosity. Those without any instructions are frightened of luminosity and try to get a body, so they wander in samsara. If you do not apprehend the luminosity, the result luminosity will arise as the yidam deity with marks and signs, which is called the pure illusory body. Tsurtön Wangi Dorje said, 'I feel for those who suffer. I do not want to depend on anyone else's mind; I want to depend upon the mind of my master, Lord Marpa. In the bardo, this nature of mind is the deity in essence, bliss in experience, and unborn in meaning.' That is the ultimate result.

"Master Ngakgi Wangchuk Drakpa Dunden posits that the ultimate buddha is form. But I have a debate with that. That's not it. That's called the pure illusory body. It empowers one hundred thousand bodhisattvas in the ten directions. After they receive the Dharma, they ultimately reach the tenth level of a bodhisattva," he said.

"What are the results of phowa?" I asked.

"The first," he said, "is when you do enforced phowa for wicked people who have committed the five heinous deeds[45] and they are born in the Formless realm. The second is when you perform phowa to choose a womb and are born as a god or human universal emperor. The third is when you do phowa through training, apprehend the result luminosity, and then awaken to buddhahood. The fourth is if you do not apprehend luminosity, you take a pure illusory body and then achieve the result of a bodhisattva on the tenth level."

"So how is it that one wanders from luminosity into the six classes of samsara?" I asked.

Those who have no instructions get frightened by the luminosity and look for a body. During the bardo of becoming, they take a mental body. That is called an impure illusory body. Its characteristic is that it arises out of the result luminosity as a mental body that takes the form of the physical body of the previous existence. Others say it arises in whatever form it will take in the next life. All its faculties are complete and it is unobstructed. Feelings are coarser than before. Unobstructed means that it can go anywhere other than the dharma expanse and the mother's womb. Though others say it is prevented from going to Bodhgaya, it is not.

Those of a similar type and those with divine eyes see it—those in the bardo and gods see it. It has powerful karmic miraculous powers, and not the miracles of wisdom. The length of time it stays in the bardo of becoming is seven days, or fourteen, twenty-one, twenty-eight, thirty-five, forty-two, or at most forty-nine days. The condition for moving to the next life is that it feels lust for the parents, enters the womb, and then feels aversion."

"It is said that there are secret mantra instructions for the treacherous path in the bardo. What are they?" I asked.

"The first is not to enter the bardo of becoming too quickly. The second is to think 'I will not enter a mother's womb' so that you do not enter a womb. The third is to recognize the result luminosity and remain within bliss," he said.

ITHI

I prostrate to the genuine gurus.

Later I received instructions from the precious lama and meditated. After a few days, there occurred vividly clear experience that came from an unidentifiable source. When I asked Rinpoche, he replied, "That is called the white panacea. In the next few days and beyond, it will always occur like this, so have a warm drape behind you, wear light clothes, and meditate. Then you will be able to make your mind workable."

Then I went to look for food since I had none and did not see him for three months. He was staying at Ölkha Sup, so I went there and spent a few days meditating. This brought on true experience of bliss, clarity, and nonthought. I asked the lama about it. He stared and then said, "Now your meditation is good. What brought it on?"

"I don't know."

"Then you need to keep meditating on just that," he said. I meditated a few more days, and the bliss and clarity occurred everywhere I went. I had the thought that it was mind. I told the lama that I was beginning to know that thoughts as well are mind. "Whatever occurs, whether bliss, clarity, warmth, or whatever it may be, meditate over and over again for short periods," he replied.

I meditated for a few days, which made an unbearable heat occur below my navel. When I asked Rinpoche, he said, "A bit of wind has got in. Since there is wind in the channels, thoughts collect there, so do not meditate on chandali itself for a few days." Even though I did not do chandali, just thinking about it made the same thing happen, so I asked about it. "All of that is thought," he replied, "So hold the breath gently below the navel and meditate on mahamudra itself. Let the winds go wherever they will."

Then one time I could not see anything—meditator, meditation, sights or sounds—and a vividly clear awareness occurred. I asked about it, and Rinpoche said, "It's said to be like the dream of a mute or the bliss of a girl; you can't learn it from explanations. You should do one meditation until you know it completely, so whenever you have questions or feel uncomfortable, come to me even if I'm in retreat."

One night I dreamt that a bhikshu came and taught some Dharma I had never heard before. It occurred clearly, so I asked about it. Rinpoche said, "Did you like it?"

"I did," I replied.

He rebuked me severely, and then said, "There are many miracles I see with my direct sight, but because I know they are all illusions, they become the path. If you cling to them as true, they are obstacles, so whatever occurs in your mind, do not embrace it, even if it is good. Do not reject it, even if it is bad. What you need to know is that they are all nondual. If you do not know that, when something undesirable happens, it will become an obstacle."

Then when heat arose through meditating on chandali, I became bound by the afflictions. I asked about it, and Rinpoche said, "That is the increase of bodhichitta taking you into bliss. You should meditate that it spreads up from the jewel of the vajra and fills everything up to your crown with bliss. Then if it seems as if the drop below will be lost, think there is an orange ma at your crown. Think that you have two eyes at your navel that are looking up at it."

Then my mind was undistracted in bliss and clarity. Even if a thought might occur, I knew it was mind, so the thought was not able to continue. I knew conceptualizations to be mind, and they were also not able to continue. I asked, and Rinpoche said, "The yogini Gayadhara said to the yogi Vajra Shri, 'Child of noble family:

> 'Don't look at objects; look at mind.
> Have few activities; get rid of all wishes.
> Do not be anxious. Needs will bind you.
> Let your mind go wherever it will.'

"When Vajra Shri achieved siddhi, he said:

> 'Nondual mind is like water mixed with milk.
> No matter what cloudlike experiences are like,
> Whatever the yogi's elephantlike mind realizes
> Permeates everything like space.
> Thus without letting awareness follow thought,
> Know whatever thought occurs to be mind.'

"That vividly clear awareness, like space, should be known to be mind. When you know everything is mind, it is said, 'The yak bull has gone to the north, but its lead rope has broken.' Thoughts are like clouds. When one arrives, more will come. These are all called experiences. Whatever occurs, know it to be mind and meditate," he said.

Then my awareness was vividly clear, and occasionally I would have the thought that there was nothing that was not my mind, from the Peak of Existence down to the mandala of wind. I asked about it, and Rinpoche replied, "As described in the Hevajra tantra, the nature is:

> There is no form, no one who sees;
> No sound nor anyone who hears;
> No scent nor anyone who smells:
> No taste nor anyone who tastes.

"So it is described as:

> Like pouring water into water,
> Like pouring oil into oil…

"So let the body and mind relax within and rest. Everything in the three realms down to the mandala of wind is mind. Nothing is inherently established," he said.

Then I asked, "Is so-called luminosity what we call knowing all phenomena to be mind?"

"When you understand everything is so, we say that our own awareness is clear and unceasing. It has no birth and cessation. That is what we call luminosity," he said.

Then when I was staying alone, I wanted from my heart to laugh. Laughter came when it was time to sleep, and I could not sleep near people. When I asked about it, he said, "That is the increase of bliss. It is good." Then one day when I asked for something to do about it, he said, "What I have always explained before is enough. If you do not meditate, you might know the bardo instructions, but it will not help. If you are still able to meditate, continuing it will be enough. During the bardo, follow that luminosity of meditation. The natural luminosity will come to welcome you."

"Is it enough if I can meditate?" I asked.

Rinpoche replied, "I call that the white panacea. Even I don't have anything else."

But then my bliss was vividly clear, and it occasionally became a means of distraction. It was clear by day but not at night. When I asked Rinpoche, he said, "You still have one fault. That one fault is that you are pleased it if it is clear and displeased if it is not. You should not do that. Let your vividly clear awareness be, and do not follow after thoughts. Whatever thought occurs, know that it is mind. You should know that mind is unborn. Whatever occurs in your mind, you should know that it is nondual. The clarity in the day is the mixture of awareness and appearance. At night as well, it is vivid bliss that is not anything at all. Sit silently where there are many people and meditate. See whether meditation occurs as well whenever you are moving about."

It became so that there was no distinction between the two. I asked, and he said, "Ah, that is it."

In the past I had done some small, minor misdeeds. When I meditated on karma and result, just remembering them made me suffer greatly. When I asked about it, Rinpoche said, "Those will all be purified by one session of emptiness.

For example, touching a spark of fire to a haystack turns it into nothing. Similarly, the minor misdeeds you have done are thoughts. They are mind. Making that mind unborn will purify them."

Then I had the thought that everything that appeared and all sounds are mind. There was nothing else. When I looked at the nature of mind, I could not contact it; it was like whirling a spear in the sky. When this occurred, I asked about it. Rinpoche replied, "Let this mind settle into its natural purity and clarity without following thoughts or correcting it. Whatever inappropriate thought occurs, do not be displeased. Look right at it. It has no color, no shape, and nothing to identify. That is the essence of awareness itself, so it is clear and unceasing."

Rinpoche had said that the periods of bliss, clarity, and nonthought should not last long, so I asked him. "In order to make them not last long," he replied, "do not say, 'Now it is clear.' When you experience great bliss in the body, if that lasts a long time during clear nonthought, the mind will be distracted by the body's bliss, so the wind will escape through all your pores and later you will get cold." He also related the story of Geshe Chen Ngawa.

Then among bliss, clarity, and nonthought, clarity was predominant for me. During those times, when my mind got distracted, it would mix with external and internal things. Then when I distinguished mind from them, I could not remember anything. When I asked, Rinpoche said, "That awareness which is clear and vivid is fundamentally mind, so do not lose that. Whatever you think of, make the mind its basis. Do not alter it. Without considering or examining, relax your body and mind within and do stupid meditation. It is said that when water is not polluted, its nature is clear; when the mind is not sullied, its nature is clear. If you consider and examine, if you correct it, or if you get attached or become averse, mind will become unclear."

Then one time my bliss decreased, but the clarity and non-thought were okay. I asked about it. "There's no fault at all. When the bliss was strong, the meditation lasted so long that it dissipated," he said.

Another time during a session of sleep, I was able to enumerate everything. At that time I felt the incredible suffering of the hungry ghosts. I asked about it. "That is a problem with the wind," he replied. "This will eliminate it," he said and taught me a profound exercise. That cleared it up.

One morning I was called into his presence, so I went. "The wind has carried the two of us away," he told me. "There would have been no way to know that from the Dharma you have studied and been taught. Only now have you found authentic Dharma. The previous appearance of the hungry ghosts was desirable. It did not come from any where else; it came from your own mind. Your mind is the unborn dharmakaya, so meditate like that," he said.

Then one time it was as if the mind was dissolving downward. When that happened, it was as if no thoughts at all could occur. I asked about it. "A small amount of wind entered the avadhuti," he said. "It won't happen all the time."

Another time I dreamt that I bored down into the depths of the earth, and it was exactly as if I had that experience. I asked, and Rinpoche replied, "We take thoughts as the path, but that does not occur through knowing trivial thoughts to be mind. However, if you have a dream or if you experience the sufferings of the lower realms, jumping into fire, jumping into water, or great suffering, go with it. Take it as the path. That finally is truly practicing the Dharma. Be very keen about this. When you look at such suffering, it has no color or shape. None of it transcends the mind. It is all mind. And the mind is unborn, so that is how you should meditate."

Then by meditating a few days, I experienced an appearance of hell. I knew it was mind and asked. Rinpoche said, "Generally, this mahayana secret mantra is profound truth. We do not cling to hell or the listener's truths. Their objects do not exist; they are confused perceptions of mind. Thus there is nothing more profound than this taking thoughts as the path, so when an experience of hell occurs again, know that it is mind. Know that mind is unborn. Through growing familiar with that, when the appearances of hells occur by and by in the bardo, you will know them to be mind and it will be like bumping into a ball of silken thread. As Master Toktsewa said:

> Because of knowing this, although it is possible
> To be reborn in hell by force of the appearances
> Caused by negative imprints,
> The hells themselves are Sukhavati.[46]
> This is the meaning of that saying.

Then once a pain occurred at the place where the three channels joined, and then there was swelling directly in front of that. The posterior fontanelle also swelled, and I had no appetite. When this happened, I asked about it. Rinpoche said, "It is a minor illness of the elements. Most illnesses of great meditators occur when thoughts slip in because the contemplation and meditation on the Dharma is not excellent. This is said to be called 'losing yourself to duality by meditating on nonduality.' All illness is just hope and fear. You are enfeebled by hopes and blocked by fears, so look at the pain itself. It has no color and no shape. Everything is mind, so do not worry about getting sick. Do not hope to get better. Think that this takes care of it."

Then my equipoise was clear and vivid. During that period, I went up to the edge of a cliff. Thinking, "This is a dream," I almost went over the precipice. When I asked about this, Rinpoche said, "The original appearance became hazy. The second was permeated by luminosity. The third was resting within the mind. There's nothing to change in any of them."

Then once there occurred a naturally clear awareness that was not anything. Other times, in contrast, nothing else was visible at all. As I made myself familiar with this, the elements dissolved in succession and I left this body. Then I asked whether that essence of awareness was the dharmakaya. "Whatever occurred, you made the mind and body into two, but they did not become two," he replied. "When everything becomes luminosity and there are no things or attributes, that is called buddha."

Then for a while I would lose consciousness for one or two periods of a few hours. I asked Rinpoche about it, and he replied, "Oh, that's the one thing you want least of all. That sort of thing is said to have deceived many in the past. It is great shamatha that merely causes rebirth as a god or human. "Meditation that is good now will dissipate in the future. Do not try to prolong this awareness because of thoughts. Thus if one thought occurs, know it is mind. If two occur, know they are mind. However many thoughts there are, when one that is undesirable occurs, direct your awareness toward it. Know that it is mind. If you are unable, relax and let it be," he said.

Then my head and upper body ached from meditating. I

wondered whether merely knowing it was mind would help and asked. "There is an important point here. Know that the pain is your mind, but when you think you need to dispel the pain, you have lapsed into using emptiness as the antidote for the afflictions. Look at the pain itself. It has no color or shape or anything that can be established as an essence. If you know that is the nature of mind, the pain has a peaceful nature."

Then for a while it was unlike anything before. There was less staying. When I directed my attention toward vivid awareness, any thought that occurred was absorbed into it. When a few thoughts occurred, the experience became even better. When I loosened my awareness, an unidentifiable experience of clarity and emptiness occurred within. In between sessions, the result was in the mind; there was nothing at all established outside of the mind. I asked, and Rinpoche said, "Ah, that's it. In The Way of the Bodhisattva it says to look a yoke's length away. If the mind gets agitated, direct your awareness clearly toward a small object that is a cubit away. Then without wanting any thought, direct awareness toward whatever occurs. If you get lethargic, rouse the mind. Then when the mind becomes compliant, it is permissible to look further away as well.

"Shamatha and resting in the nature of the mind itself are not the same. Shamatha is to not think of anything at all. Resting in the nature of the mind itself means that when you direct awareness, any thought that occurs becomes the expe rience of clarity and emptiness; it is not a problem if it lasts a while. This is called awareness going out the door. Generally it is called all-pervasive awareness."

Then when I was holding the gentle breath, there was nothing to truly hold but there was a lot of heat. I asked about it, and he replied, "The winds have been trained until they are pure. It's good. Meditating like that is enough. However, do not get distracted by awareness itself. As Tsochik said, 'Nothing can harm me, but the wish to move instead of stay naturally gets stronger.' When that happens, the problems multiply. However, we two are still attracted by talk. We need to keep meditating."

"When focusing your awareness," I asked, "if the clear emptiness where no thing at all is seen lasts a long time, will that create any faults?"

Rinpoche replied, "If it lasts too long, there is a taint of stagnation and lethargy. So disrupt it by slackening. Loosen and relax. Then the experience of clear emptiness with neither inside nor outside will occur. So keep meditating."

At that time, an unidentifiable experience of clear emptiness occurred, so I asked about it. "That is what is called the nondual pristine wisdom of a buddha's mind. We know it is just that," he said.

Then one time it was clear yet without any focus, and that became groundless. I asked about it. "That is called the essence of the ultimate natural state itself. Similarly, whatever painful thing occurs, direct the awareness toward it so that it becomes groundless. That is dharma nature. Similarly, whatever arises—spirits, magic, and so forth—direct your awareness right at it," he said.

I asked what the difference was between directing the awareness toward things that are near and things that are far. "When the mind is agitated, direct the mind toward a small thing that is close by," he replied. "If torpid, you should direct the mind toward a small thing that is up high."

Then one time when I was meditating, occasionally there were no things at all that I could describe and it was just merely empty. I asked about it. "All of that is just differences in experiences. While teachers of the middle way, mind only, transcendent wisdom, mantra, and other schools may have their own assertions, the fulfillment of those intentions is the same. There is not a single thing that is not contained within mind."

I had the thought that merely remaining vividly within bliss and clarity alone would definitely lead to rebirth as a god or human. "This coemergent union of ours is a profound instruction. Whatever thought occurs, whatever undesirable thing occurs, know it to be mind. This is training the mind so that everything and anything you do is just a dream and an illusion."

Then once I directed my awareness vividly toward different things one at a time and then relaxed and loosened, letting it be. There were not any things at all; it was gentle and calm within clear emptiness itself. At that time, wherever I wanted to go, it was as if there were no walls or mountains. I asked about this. "Oh, that experience of yours is most excellent," he replied. "First, the view is this vividly clear awareness. This is the great nondual pristine wisdom, the mind of all the buddhas. Due to it, meditation has brought you grad ually up the steps through which you needed to progress. Another hundred and thousand more like that will come," he said.

Dialogues between Rinpoche Gampopa and Rinpoche Dusum Khyenpa. May this Dharma benefit sentient beings.

The Final Words of Dusum Khyenpa

I prostrate to the Omniscient One, the Lord of Dharma, Dusum Khyenpa, whose name is as famous as the sun and moon. He gave his final words in the Year of the Ox during the daytime on the first day of the tiger (or first) month. As his physical form was fading, he gathered to him a few of the senior monks including Geshe Tsangpowa, Pöndul, Pön Drakseng, Drakrin, Könchok Gyaltsen, and Na Ünpa. To them he gave his final words:

"What I have kept for myself are the clothes that cover my body and a stone mill for grinding roasted barley. Everything else belongs to the Sangha. Five of you should take possession of the two hundred twenty-two gold sang, the silver and turquoise, silk brocade, dzo, horses, and everything in the kitchen. Use them to benefit the monks who do retreat. After I depart, stay here for one or two years."

Pön Drakseng asked, "How long should we stay?"

Rinpoche straightened his body and opened his eyes wide, "At the least, wouldn't it be for one or two summers and winters? Also, Shönnu, you stay here one or two years. Do not lose so much as a single letter from the representations of body, speech, and mind related to my practice. I will also give a command and entrust them to the Dharma protectors."

For three months beginning that night, many impressive signs appeared continuously—rainbows in the sky, earthquakes, and roaring sounds. In particular, as the night of the second moved into the third day of the month, earthquakes shuddered unceasingly and rainbow parasols floated above the monastery. Some people saw crowds of dakinis, heard the sounds of damarus, and so forth. After breakfast on the third, the monks were allowed to come and see Dusum Khyenpa. Then he said, "Now go," straightened his body, sat in vajra posture, and looked for a long time into space. Covering his head with part of his robes, he entered into his final meditation. On the evening of the third day, when the sun and moon came close together, at the age of eighty-four he left for another world realm to benefit beings.

During the cremation on the tenth day of the month, people saw many different phenomena. In the same way for everyone present, the sun appeared to stay twice as long as usual. Some people saw thirteen, eight, or seven suns, which coalesced and separated. The sun's rays took the shape of a parasol fashioned of peacock feathers. Dakas and dakinis clad in bone ornaments came into view. It rained flowers. Rainbow parasols floated in tiers above the cremation stupa. The smoke transformed into rainbows in which Dusum Khyenpa appeared. Flights of birds circled around the rising smoke. The sounds from the fire resonated in beautiful tones. Wild animals gathered to pay their respects. Those not engaged in spiritual activity became engaged;

those already engaged developed their practice further.

In the cremation stupa, he left behind relics for the benefit of others: his heart, which was emptiness and compassion inseparable, his tongue, which had taught the Dharma of different vehicles, and the relics that came from perfect training in bodhichitta. Due to his attainment of stability in the creation stage, numerous images of deities appeared as well.

After he passed away, most of the monks had dispersed by the winter of the new year. In the spring, those who remained included Geshe Tsangpowa, Sherjung, Könseng, Pön Rinchen Senge, and Pön Drakseng. Entrusted with the care of the main seat, this core group of monks met to discuss the situation. They all thought that Tsurphu was difficult to maintain and hard for people to reach. In general they also agreed that Chara would be suitable for the main seat because it was in the heart of the country and easily accessible by road.

They asked Gomdar to be the manager and then gathered at Chara. From Tau Rinchen Gang came a master artist who was skilled in making reliquary stupas. Geshe Töngyal invited Geshe Nyelde, a master in the craft of making earthen stupas. All of the work of creating the stupas was given over to them. Geshe Yorpo was put in charge of laying out the foundation for the offering chamber to be erected on top of an existing building.

At that time, Master Sherrin said, "Listen here, you two. Rinpoche turned his thoughts to Tsurphu Monastery and came here from Kampo Nenang. Here, he gathered a community of monks and bestowed his final words. Here, he passed away and here, too, his body was cremated. During his meditations here, he had many clear visions of deities and performed numerous empowerments and consecrations. If you leave this blessed land, where would you go?"

So the master and two disciples made a commitment. They would blend ashes from the cremation with milk, perfume, and other precious substances and make them into a statue of Dusum Khyenpa. Inside would be placed relics from the Buddha, remains from the previous Kagyu lamas, and relics from the remains of Rinpoche, the Lord of Dharma, as well as his hair, fingernails, toenails, robes, and so forth. When the statue was completely finished, it would be placed in his former sleeping quarters to inspire devotion.

They wished to build a reliquary stupa so that the ashes and so forth from the cremation would not deteriorate. The leaders and disciples discussed this at length. Among the many traditions of building stupas, they decided to build an earthen one resembling the Glorious Drepung Stupa.

In this Rose Apple Continent there are representations of the three kayas that are most wondrous. In southern India is the dharmakaya representation, the Glorious Drepung Stupa, which has an umbrella that does not touch the stupa. The divine artist Vishvakarman created the stupa, and it was sponsored by four great gods. In the outer ocean is the sambhogakaya representation, a statue of glorious Vairochana Gangchentso, which is crafted from five different jewels. On the crown of his head is a large water crystal offered by Rahula. The statue itself was created by Vishvakarman. In Bodhgaya is the nirmanakaya representation, a statue imbued with perfume made from a special white sandalwood. Fashioned by Vishvakarman and sponsored by the youngest brother of a Brahmin family, it represents the Buddha at thirty-eight and has jewel eyes.

Later, Nyima Nyingpo, a pandita who resided at Drepung Stupa, called an artist from eastern India. He made a great painting that showed the stupa's precise form, the exact arrangement of the deities in the vase section, and how the life story of Nagarjuna is arranged around it. The pandita then carried this thangka to Tibet and gave it to his two disciples who were Dharma teachers.

Hearing that the thangka was now in the temple erected by Geshe Len, Geshe Namparwa's nephew, who was a teacher, went to Lhasa along with others to give offerings and make a copy of the thangka. They studied the plastering and the measurements of the stupa from Geshe Namparwa's disciple Belbu Lotsawa, who had gone to India twice from Lhasa's Tango area. They then returned to Tsurphu.

Previously, Rinpoche had said, "Here behind our monastery build a Drepung Stupa and circumambulate it," so they had the spiritual authority to build one. In the place where his body had been cremated, they consecrated the ground for this stupa in a ceremony of five stages. On that day, there was a great snowfall and the sky was filled with rainbows shaped like parasols. They appeared from that day onward until the stupa was finished.

At the monastery, they meditated on bodhichitta for the humans and nonhumans who create obstacles to virtuous activity. They wore the armor of patience to turn aside the blows of verbal weapons. In order to fulfill the wishes of the precious lama—the essential nature of all the buddhas—Master Sherrin generated bodhichitta and took his measuring stick in hand. After I completed the walls, in ten days I finished the construction of the stupa all the way up to the plinth resting on top of the vase section.

Gyalpo Dorje Drak was called to do the fine plaster finish, and in half a month the work was done. Looking like a perfect metal casting, or bas-relief, of the original image, the stupa was completed in twenty-five days. Everyone who saw it said, "Magnificent!"

Within the stupa were relics of the buddhas; a bone of the Tathagata Langpo; leaves and buds from the Bodhi Tree; earth from the eight great places; and eleven cast-metal statues from Khotan, the foremost of which was an eighteen-inch statue of the glorious Khasarpani. There were many representations of speech, such as two volumes (written in gold), and many others. From Rinpoche they placed in the stupa his hair, bones, relics, fingernails, toenails, his robes, cushion, and footprints. From previous Kagyu masters there were bones, hair, and innumerable other precious objects.

Resting on the plinth above the vase section were thirteen levels of vajra wheels. Placed above them was a copper cover, which was made by the expert smith Triten to protect the stupa from rain. The faithful disciple Mutsu Agtsom went to Nepal and brought back a gold spire, which was installed. Everything turned out just as the artist had depicted, and everyone found the stupa wondrous. In Tibet it became famous as the template for anyone who wanted to construct a Glorious Drepung Stupa.

Endowed with blessings, this excellent artistic support for

Dharma practice was the field for the accumulation of merit by close and devoted disciples including Geshe Marpa and Geshe Dren. Since this had gone so well, four cotton-clad yogis who were great meditators built a reliquary chamber to contain the relics of Rinpoche's heart and tongue.

The two bhikshus Rongpa (uncle and nephew) along with other monks, and the yogi practitioner Gompa Repa along with other yogis had tremendous loyalty to the main seat of Tsurphu and kept their minds stable and focused. These great leonine meditators concentrated on practice and rested evenly in one-pointed meditative concentration. All of them gathered together and with immense devotion stayed at Tsurphu.

Twenty-one years after the stupa was built, Tsangpowa, the glory of living beings, was serving as the lama for the Dharma king of Minyak. Tsangpowa repeatedly paid his respects to this main seat of Tsurphu, which resembles Bodhgaya. He offered inconceivably precious articles, such as representations of body, speech, and mind plus the five varieties of jewels and silk brocades. In particular, he offered a coating mixed with gold to the Drepung Stupa and provided all that was needed for the task, including the artisans who were sent from Minyak Gha.

In order to fill all their intentions, Geshe Shenshen Tönge and Gompa Dorje Jangchup sponsored the care of the artisans, and the kind-hearted Gompa Köntsul took the role of the manager. The one who did the work on the stupa was a close attendant of Rinpoche named Shönnu, who was generally skilled in the various arts and particularly adept at building stupas. Once the surface of the stupa was well prepared, the artisans from Gha offered the coating mixed with gold.

All the monks living at the main seat, old and young alike, were inspired by faith and joyous diligence. The stupa was spacious, like an infinite palace: the four gates had their protectors and the four kings resided in their abodes on the terraces. It was eight armspans around with sides of equal length. Once the walls were finished, they called from Dechen Sölnak Tangpoche a talented youth who was very skilled in plastering, a shining example of his craft. The plaster was made from silver and the color shone silver as well. It was all finished in two years.

A curved roof of azure blue tiles crafted by Tsul Kyap, a skilled artisan, was placed above the stupa to protect it from rain, functioning as an ornamental shield. For its peak, Chungpo Pön Josey sent a considerable amount of funds to a Nepalese craftsperson to make a spire. It was brought from far away to Tsurphu and set as the central ornament of the stupa, making it a radiant place at the monastery.

Everyone who saw the stupa, knowledgeable and ordinary alike, said that this great work of art was most excellent. Like a glorious banner, its fame spread to every country under the sun. It became the template for all those building stupas from up in Balpo Dobik to Minyak Gha. Disciples and patrons came from all directions to pay their respects and make offerings. Afterward, when they supplicated, all their goals, both relative and ultimate, were accomplished just as they had wished. It has become a great reliquary stupa, a precious wish-fulfilling gem, providing everything needed and wished for as long as the Buddha's teachings remain.

Anniversary Poem

by His Holiness the Seventeenth Karmapa,
Ogyen Trinley Dorje

like nectar streaming down from a spring on a snowy
mountain face,
from some highest of realms high above,
with effortless vigor and a deep, unprompted longing,
drop after divine drop, each pristine and pure,
you crossed the mountains and plains of hundreds of
months and years,
to come cascading down, down into the land of our
hopes.
coursing through deep aspirations you held, held
through the stream of many lives,
from some place completely obscured to us, you gave
gentle warmth and nourished us.
since then, the tender young sprouts of virtuous minds
have blossomed with leaves and fruit,
and land once scorched with drought burst into life
turquoise-green.
when a snow lion roars on a white mountain peak
the sound at once sends the crisp flakes swirling
in a flurry.
when you arrived in the year eleven-ten

the lion's roar of your majestic name blazed forth,
spreading its unchanging splendor and unequalled
blessings.
day and night, for nine hundred years,
it has set trembling the hearts of those with faith, scared
away the sleep of our ignorance
and stilled the waves of thought that trouble the ocean
of our minds.
because you are here, we dare to face the angry
countenance of the samsaric sea.
because you are here, we know that there is an end to
this suffering.
the world, its voice raised in cries of birth and death,
falls silent.
your deeds blend completely with a sky as deep blue as
your brilliant crown.
your great heart, like a splendid mandala of wind,
keeps this world ever moved.

O Karmapa, you who act,
I am all that you have. and you are all that I have.

Notes

1. According to some scriptures, the Buddhist teachings will remain in this world for ten periods of 500 years after the Buddha passed away. In each of those periods, the teachings will grow progressively weaker.

2. Shantarakshita's *Ornament of the Middle Way,* Yeshe Nyingpo's *Two Truths in the Middle Way*, and Kamalashila's *Illumination of the Middle Way.*

3. This song appears on page 210.

4. This song appears on page 218.

5. The eastern pure land of the Buddha Akshobhya.

6. Another name for Dusum Khyenpa.

7. Nonhuman, formless beings.

8. That is, virtuous actions that lead to positive karmic results within samsara but not to liberation or omniscience.

9. The first of the hot hells, where beings are killed and then immediately revived, only to be killed again.

10. That is, the Dharma of the foundation vehicle, which removes the afflictions but not all the stains of their imprints.

11. Respectively, the miraculous powers, the noble eightfold path, tranquillity and insight meditation, and achieving arhatship and nirvana.

12. Atisha was a member of the Mahasanghika tradition of the vinaya, but Tibetans were all members of the Mulasaravastivada tradition.

13. "Protector" usually refers to Mahakala.

14. As explained in *A String of Jewels*, he also saw Gomtsul as a form of light, thus making six pure visions.

15. This song appears on page 210.

16. This song appears on page 212.

17. A kriya tantra based on Amoghapasha, a form of Avalokiteshvara.

18. The text says only "de nyid" for Bhagavan Guhyasamaja; however, this full name is given in sKyabs rje mkhan chen khra 'gu rin po che [and sMan sdong bla ma rin po che karma nges don bstan rgyas], *dPal rgyal dbang Karma pa sku phreng bcu drug pa tshun rim par byon pa'i rnam thar phyogs bsgrigs*, p. 165.

19. The text here gives only "One-Faced," but "Jetsunma" is found just after the previous quotation in ibid., pp. 165–66.

20. The names of the others are not mentioned here explicitly but can be inferred from the text. One was Master Sherrin, who studied the measurements and "took his measuring stick in hand" (see the second paragraph below), and another was the author, Bhikshu Kumara Bodhi, who studied plastering and built the walls. In that same paragraph he refers to himself, saying, "After I completed the walls, I finished..."

21. The author, Bhikshu Kumara Bodhi, is speaking here of himself.

22. The text literally reads "one armspan with equal sides," but it seems to be corrupted here. "Eight armspans" is found in both *The Final Words* and in the account of the stupa found in Rin chen dpal bzang, *mTshur phu dgon gyi dkar chag kun gsal me long*, p. 125.

23. Someone with deep meditation experience no longer needs formal spiritual training, and continuing to use contrived methods of practice would actually hinder their resting in meditation. Thus training is an adversary for such practitioners even though it is necessary for beginners.

24. Lesser individuals are motivated to achieve happiness in the next life; middling individuals wish to achieve their own liberation from samsara; and greater individuals wish to awaken to buddhahood for the benefit of all beings.

25. The hundred-syllable purificatory mantra of Vajrasattva.

26. A night-blooming water lily, *Nymphaea esculenta.*

27. The four traits are not to criticize even when criticized, not to get angry even at those who are angry at you, not to strike even those who strike you, and not to point out faults even when yours are pointed out.

28. Here the Tibetan text uses this Sanskrit word, which means suffering.

29. Faults that arise in meditation due to attachment to meditative experiences of bliss, clarity, and nonthought.

30. Straying from uncontrived meditation due to intellectual understanding and the three types of meditative experiences.

31. The flower of a tree (*Ficus racemosa*) that, according to Buddhist literature, blooms only once every several thousand years.

32. That is, the ultimate buddha nature of the buddhas, who are self-arisen in that they are primordially and spontaneously present and not produced by causes or conditions.

33. Since engaging in conduct requires a very high view, this could mean that he had the view and knowledge but did not engage in all the conduct that a siddha might. Alternatively, it could also be an instance of the tradition of putting oneself down and not boasting about one's realization.

34. These two stanzas refer to masters of the Kadampa lineage.

35. The preceding four stanzas refer to Gampopa.

36. Validity (*tshad ma*) is the study of what makes a cognition reliable and valid.

37. The oral transmission of teachings given during the time of Guru Rinpoche and preserved in the Nyingma tradition.

38. The *People's Doha*, *Queens' Doha*, and *King's Doha* by Saraha.

39. A blue lotus flower, Nympheaea caerulea.

40. Vajrapani.

41. The story is related in chapter 13 of The Golden Isle on pages 31.

42. It appears that a line is missing here in the original text.

43. The smaller words in italics are annotations by either the author or a later Tibetan editor.

44. The six buddhas who each perform their activity in the six classes of samsara: Shakra, Vemichitra, Shakyamuni, Steadfast Lion, Blazing Mouth, and Dharmaraja.

45. The five deeds that would otherwise result in taking the next rebirth in the lowest of hells, the Incessant Hell: killing one's father, killing one's mother, killing an arhat, drawing blood from the Tathagata with malicious intent, and causing a schism in the Sangha.

46. The pure realm of the buddha Amitabha.

Glossary

ABBOT. The senior monk who gives the monastic vows. It can also refer to the head of a monastery.

ACHALA. The Unshakable One, a wrathful deity. Called *Miyowa* in Tibetan.

AKANISHTA. A pure realm that is highest abode of the Desire and Form realms. Called *Okmin* in Tibetan.

ĀLI and KĀLI. The vowels and consonants of the Sanskrit alphabet, representing the sounds from which all speech and mantra derive.

ALL-ENCOMPASSING SAMADHIS. Ten types of samadhi that cause a visualized form to pervade the focus of one's meditation. The ten are earth, water, fire, air, space, and consciousness plus blue, yellow, red, and white.

AMRITA KUNDALINI. A wrathful deity who dispels obstacles. Called *Dutsi Khyilwa* in Tibetan.

ATISHA. The Indian scholar who brought the Kadampa

lineage to Tibet. Also known as Jowo Atisha and Atisha Dipamkara, 982–1054.

AVADHUTI. Also called the central channel, this is the channel for the subtle energy of body and mind that runs from the crown of the head to just below the navel.

AVALOKITESHVARA. The deity who embodies the compassion of all the buddhas. Called *Chenrezik* in Tibetan.

BARDO. The period between death and the next rebirth when the consciousness of the deceased individual experiences various appearances which come from past karma.

BHIKSHU. A fully ordained monk.

BHUTA. A type of malicious spirit.

BODHICHITTA. The resolve to achieve enlightenment for the sake of others. There are two types. Aspirational bodhichitta is the wish to achieve enlightenment, and engaged bodhichitta is actually engaging in the practices of the six paramitas and so forth in order to attain enlightenment.

BODHISATTVA LEVELS. The ten progressive levels of realization attained by a bodhisattva.

BOUNTIFUL COW. The western continent in this world system according to traditional cosmology.

BUDDHA KASHYAPA. The buddha who appeared in this world many thousands of years prior to the Buddha Shakyamuni. Called *Ösung* in Tibetan.

CHANDALI. One of the six yogas of Naropa, a practice that produces experiences of heat, bliss, and nonthought.

CLAIRVOYANCE. Six types of supernatural knowledge or sublime states of perception: performing miracles, divine sight, divine hearing, recollecting former lives, knowing others' minds, and, for great practitioners, knowing that the defilements are exhausted.

CREATION AND COMPLETION STAGES. Two phases of vajrayana practice. The emphasis of the creation phase is meditating on yidam deities to bring stability of mind. The completion phase consists of practices that entail effort such as the six yogas of Naropa and effortless practices such as mahamudra.

DAKAS AND DAKINIS. Wisdom dakas and dakinis are respectively male and female tantric deities. There are also mundane dakas and dakinis.

DAKLHA GAMPO. The main monastic seat of Gampopa. *Dwags lha sgam po.*

DAMARU. A small two-headed hand drum.

DHARMA EXPANSE. The expanse of all phenomena, or *dharmadhatu.*

DHARMAKAYA. *See* kayas.

DHARMA NATURE. The emptiness nature of all phenomena, or *dharmata.*

DHARMAS OF MAITREYA, FIVE. Five major texts given by Maitreya to Asanga, who wrote them down, composed explanations of them, and taught them. They are studied in all the Tibetan traditions.

DHYANAS. Deep states of shamatha meditation.

DIPAMKARA. Refers both to Jowo Atisha and to a buddha from a prior age whom the Buddha Shakyamuni served when he was a bodhisattva.

DORJE PALTSEK. The protector of Kampo Nenang. Sometimes called the *genyen* or local spirit. *rDo rje dpal brtsegs.*

DRE. A little more than a half kilo, or approximately one and a quarter pounds.

DUḤKHA. Sanskrit for *suffering.*

DZO. A cross between a yak and a cow, known for its strength.

EIGHT WORLDLY CONCERNS. Concern with gain and loss, pleasure and pain, fame and obscurity, and praise and blame.

ESSENCE KAYA. *See* kayas.

FIVE AREAS OF KNOWLEDGE. Buddhist philosophy, logic, grammar, medicine, and arts and crafts.

FORM KAYAS. *See* kayas.

FOUNDATION VEHICLE. The teachings of the Buddha stressing the four noble truths and the practice of discipline.

FOUR ACTIVITIES. Activities of pacifying, enriching, magnetizing, and destroying that are manifested through accomplishing vajrayana practice.

FOUR MEANS OF NURTURING DISCIPLES. Methods by which bodhisattvas gather and care for their disciples: being generous, speaking pleasantly, acting in accord with the students' needs, and acting consistently with what you teach.

GALO. Both teacher and disciple of Dusum Khyenpa and author of *The Golden Isle* and *The Spiritual Biography in Verse*. *rGa lo*.

GAMPO. Another name for Daklha Gampo. *sGam po*.

GAMPOPA. One of Milarepa's two main disciples and Dusum Khyenpa's principal teacher. *sGam po pa*, 1079–1153.

GESHE. A spiritual friend, or kalyanamitra. Often part of a teacher's name. In later centuries, this also came to refer to masters in the Geluk tradition.

GESHE CHAPA. A great scholar and teacher of Dusum Khyenpa. *Phywa pa chos kyi senge*, 1109–1169.

GOING FORTH. The first step in becoming a monk or a nun; the formal procedure for leaving one's home to enter the homeless life of a monastic.

GOMCHUNG. An early Kadampa master. *Kha rag sgom chung.*

GOMTSUL. Also referred to as Gomtsul Tsultrim Nyingpo, or Gompa. A nephew of Gampopa and one of his main disciples. *sGompa or sGom tshul tshul khrims snying po*, 1116–1169.

GREAT PERFECTION. A tradition of meditating on the nature of the mind. Called *Dzogchen* in Tibetan.

GUARDIAN PAIR. The protectors Bernakchen and Palden Lhamo.

HAYAGRIVA. The wrathful aspect of Amithaba, the Buddha of Infinite Light. Called *Tadrin* in Tibetan.

HERUKA. A name used for semi-wrathful male tantric deities such as Hevajra and Chakrasamvara.

HEVAJRA. A yidam deity of Anuttara yoga tantra.

ILLUSORY BODY. One of the six yogas of Naropa; this practice involves meditating on the illusory nature of the body and all other forms.

INSIGHT. Seeing into the true nature of mind.

JETSUN. An honorific title for males.

JETSUNMA. An honorific title for females. Often refers to Vajra Yogini or Tara.

KADAMPA. The Buddhist tradition stemming from Atisha and emphasizing the development of compassion through mind training. It was incorporated into the Kagyu tradition by Gampopa. *bKa' gdams pa.*

KAMPO NENANG. Founded in 1164 and located in Eastern Tibet, it is the first monastery established by Dusum Khyenpa. In terms of body, speech, and mind, it relates to his body. *Kam po gnas nang.*

KAYAS. The bodies of a buddha. The first is the dharmakaya, or "body of qualities," which is the qualities of a buddha's wisdom, love, and power. As its essence is wisdom, it is only perceived by the buddhas. Since others cannot perceive the dharmakaya, buddhas manifest two different kinds of form kayas. The sambhogakaya, or enjoyment body, is visible to only those beings on high bodhisattva levels who have pure perception. The nirmanakaya, or emanation body, can be perceived by ordinary beings with impure perception. An example of a nirmanakaya would be Buddha Shakyamuni; an example of a sambhogakaya would be Avalokiteshvara. Sometimes the buddhas are also described as having a fourth kaya, the essence kaya (svabhavikakaya), which is described alternately as the union of the three kayas or as their empty nature.

KEY INSTRUCTIONS. Specific instructions on key points of meditation, given by a lama based on texts or personal experience.

KHAMPA GRAY HAIR. A nickname for Dusum Khyenpa: "The Gray-Haired One from Eastern Tibet."

KHASARPANI. A two-armed manifestation of Avalokiteshvara.

KHECHARI. The name of the pure realm of Vajra Varahi. It also refers to a form of Varahi.

KURUKULLE. A wrathful form of Red Tara.

LISTENERS. The *shravakas*, or disciples of the Buddha who follow the teachings of the foundation vehicle with the goal of nirvana and freedom from samsara.

LORD OF DHARMA. A title given to great lamas. In this text, it usually refers to Gampopa.

MAHAMUDRA. "The great seal," an Indian tradition of meditating directly on the nature of mind. In Tibet it became a major practice of the Kagyu tradition.

MAHAYANA. The "great vehicle," the teachings of the second and third turnings of the Wheel of Dharma emphasizing compassion, emptiness, and Buddha nature.

MAITREYA. The future buddha, now residing in the realm of Tushita.

MAITRIPA. The Indian master who taught mahamudra to Marpa. *Me tri pa*, 1007–ca. 1085.

MAMOS. Semi-divine beings who sometimes act as Dharma protectors.

MARPA. The Tibetan translator who went to India three times to study with Naropa, Maitripa, and many other great masters. He realized the full meaning of mahamudra and several major tantras and brought these teachings back to Tibet, where he taught them. He is the primary source for most of the Kagyu lineages. *Mar pa*, 1012–1097.

MILAREPA. The wandering yogi of Tibet, famous for his songs of realization treasured by all the lineages. *Mi la ras pa*, 1040–1123.

MÖN. A mountainous kingdom to the southeast of Tibet. *Mon*.

NAIRATMYA. The main consort of Hevajra. Called *Dakmema* in Tibetan.

NIRMANAKAYA. *See* kayas.

NOVICE MONK. A monk who holds ten precepts. Usually this is a stage of training before taking full ordination.

PADMASAMBHAVA. Revered in Tibet as a second buddha, he was a fully awakened master of tantra from India and mainly responsible for the spread of vajrayana Buddhism in Tibet. Called Guru Rinpoche or Pema Jungne in Tibetan. 8th century.

PALDEN LHAMO. A female wrathful deity associated with Mahakala.

PANDITA. Sanskrit for scholar.

PARAMITAS. The six transcendent qualities of generosity, discipline, patience, diligence, meditation, and wisdom. They are so called because they transcend ordinary, worldly generosity and so forth.

PATH AND FRUITION. Teachings on the gradual path of practice that leads to the fruition of full awakening.

PATH OF METHOD. Practices that rely on the skillful means of visualization and the use of attributes.

PEAK OF EXISTENCE. The level of the highest rebirth in the Formless realm with the most subtle meditation and consciousness. Though it is considered the highest level in the world, it is still mundane and impermanent.

PHOWA. A practice for ejecting one's consciousness at the time of death in order to take rebirth in a pure realm.

PHYSICIAN OF DAKPO. *See* Gampopa.

RAHULA. A deity who creates obstacles.

RECHUNGPA. He and Gampopa were the two main disciples of Milarepa. *Ras chung pa*, 1084–1161.

ROSE APPLE CONTINENT. The continent in the south of this world system.

SADHANA. A meditation practice in several stages that leads to the realization of a deity.

SAMADHI. Concentration and deep meditative states.

SAMBHOGAKAYA. *See* kayas.

SANG. A traditional unit of money in Tibet.

SARAHA. Famous for his songs of realization and teachings on mahamudra, this mahasiddha is an important forefather in the Kagyu lineage. *Sa ra ha*, late 8th or early 9th century.

SECRET MANTRA. Another name for the vajrayana, the practice of tantric Buddhism.

SELF-BUDDHA. Self-buddhas, or *pratyekabuddhas*, are practitioners who awaken to nirvana without relying on a teacher in their last lifetime. Their realization is said to be greater than a listener's but less than a buddha's.

SEVEN BRANCHES. A method to gather the accumulation of merit by prostrating, offering, confessing, rejoicing, requesting the buddhas to teach, supplicating them to remain without passing to nirvana, and dedicating the merit to the benefit of all beings.

SHAMATHA. The meditation of resting the mind calmly and stably. Often translated as tranquillity meditation.

SIDDHI. Accomplishment that comes through practice. Ordinary siddhis are those on the mundane level, such as swift walking and invisibility. The supreme siddhi is full awakening.

SIX CLASSES OF BEINGS. Hell beings, hungry ghosts, animals, humans, demigods, and gods.

SIX CONSCIOUSNESSES. The five sensory consciousnesses and the mental consciousness.

SIX YOGAS OF NAROPA. Sometimes called simply the six yogas. These are six types of completion-stage practice that are used to enhance the practice of mahamudra: chandali, illusory body, dream yoga, luminosity, phowa, and bardo.

SUGATA. An epithet for a buddha. Literally, "one who has gone to bliss."

TANTRAS. Teachings given by the buddhas in various forms at different times and locations. They generally emphasize methods for meditating to realize our inherent buddha nature. In the tradition of the Sarma (new translations), there are four classes of tantra: the action, conduct, yoga, and unexcelled yoga tantra. The unexcelled tantra also has three aspects: the father tantra which emphasizes means, the mother tantra which emphasizes wisdom, and the nondual tantras.

TARA THE WISH-FULFILLING WHEEL. A form of Tara known as a deity of long life.

TELOPA. Forefather of the Kagyu lineage, he is famous for his direct encounter with Vajradhara and for his profound instructions such as *The Ganges Mahamudra. Te lo pa,* 988–1069.

TEN NONVIRTUES. Killing, stealing, sexual misconduct, lying, harsh speech, divisive speech, idle chatter, covetousness, malice, and wrong view.

THREE BASKETS. The three collections of the Buddha's teachings: the vinaya, sutras, and abhidharma.

TORMA. A sculpted offering made of roast barley flour, butter, and other edible substances.

TSATSA. A small clay figure made from a mold as part of a devotional practice.

TSURPHU. Located in Central Tibet in the Dowolung Valley, Tsurphu is the last monastery founded by Dusum Khyenpa in 1189. Of his body, speech, and mind, it relates to his mind. *mTshur phu.*

TUSHITA. A divine realm where a future buddha awaits the right time to take rebirth. Called *Ganden* in Tibetan.

TWO WISDOMS. The wisdom that knows the nature of all phenomena and the wisdom that knows the variety in which they manifest.

UDDIYANA. Famous as the birthplace of Guru Rinpoche and for a flourishing tantric practice, it is said to be located in the Swat Valley of northwest India, though some scholars say that it includes a much larger area. Called *Ogyen* in Tibetan.

VAJRA POSTURE. The full lotus posture.

VAJRA VARAHI. A wisdom dakini and the consort of Chakrasamvara.

VAJRA YOGINI. Another name for Vajra Varahi.

WHITE TARA. *See* Tara the Wish-Fulfilling Wheel.

YAKSHAS. A class of demons, often described as the henchmen of Yama, the Lord of Death.

YAMANTAKA. The fearsome one; a wrathful manifestation of Manjushri.

YIDAM. A meditational deity.

YOGIC CONDUCT. *See* yogic discipline.

YOGIC DISCIPLINE. The conduct of a great meditator who has developed a high realization and wants to test it in worldly situations.

Bibliography

sKyabs rje mkhan chen khra 'gu rin po che [and sMan sdong bla ma rin po che karma nges don bstan rgyas]. *dPal rgyal dbang karma pa sku phreng bcu drug pa tshun rim par byon pa'i rnam thar phyogs bsgrigs.* Sarnath, India: Vajra Vidya Library, 2008.

rGyal dbang karma pa dus gsum mkhyen pa. *rGyal dbang karma pa dus gsum mkhyen pa'i gsung thor bu.* Gangtok, Sikkim, India: Dzongsar Chhentse Labrang, 1980. http://www.tbrc.org/#library_work_Object-W23651

dPa' bo gtsug lag phreng ba. Chos *'byung mkhas pa'i dga' ston*, vol 2. Sarnath, India: Vajra Vidya Library, 2003.

Rin chen dpal bzang. *mTshur phu dgon gyi dkar chag kun gsal me long*. Beijing: Mi rigs dpe skrun khang, 1995.

Si tu chos kyi *'byung gnas. bKa' brgyud gser phreng rnam thar zla ba chu shel gyi phreng ba*, vol. 1. Sarnath, India: Vajra Vidya Library, 2004.

May all beings be happy